COLLIDE

Exploring INTERGenerational
Ministry

By Tammy Tolman
2013

Scripture taken from THE MESSAGE. Copyright © 1993, 1994, 1995, 1996, 2000, 2001, 2002. Used by permission of NavPress Publishing Group.

ISBN 978-0-9875390-0-7

Cover design by Bluestone Design

Typeset by Wes Selwood, selwood media & design

Printed in Australia by Creative Visions Print and Design

Contents

Acknowledgements

I would like to acknowledge Freshhope ministries (Churches of Christ in NSW), the community where I have been allowed to grow, felt safe to explore and within which I have endeavoured to faithfully serve God. I have been a part of this community all my life and have loved the partnership as together we seek to serve in God's purposes. Freshhope is all about facilitating transformational communities of fresh hope. I am blessed to have been a part of a movement which has given me wings to fly and also provided a safe place to rest. I have worked within Freshhope ministries on a local and state level also representing them on a national level for over 20 years. During the past 10 years in particular, I have had the wonderful support of Andrew Ball and John Crowther. I thank them for their godly leadership and encouragement to stay the course, even when the course was not always clear. Freshhope ministries has a heart for families and children and has always wanted to support and encourage transformational ministry at the local and state level. They have always sought to provide support and resources for this ministry, where in many other denominations children have been overlooked. So on behalf of children and families, I thank you.

Tammy

Dedications

David Tolman: my husband and best friend

The journey of this book has not been travelled alone. Although I have written it, we have lived every aspect of what it means to holistically collide together. We are a mighty team and I could not be in ministry if it wasn't for the support of my husband in every way. I dedicate this book to him as our "collision" in marriage has been the best experience of what it means to bring a piece of heaven down to earth. We are truly partners on the journey together as we endeavour to create environments where the generations can collide. I love him very much and look forward to more "collisions" in the future together.

Sam and Georgia Tolman: my children

I have two amazing children to "collide" with every day. They keep me honest, sane, and humble. They make me laugh and sometimes cry, but I am always thankful to walk with them on this journey. They amaze me with their talents, their heart to serve and the willingness they have to go on the adventure of full time ministry with me wherever that takes us all.

I Central 316: our Faith Community

We began "colliding" together in 2005. I have been in ministry for twenty-four years, and the last seven years have truly been some of the best. I don't think of being the lead pastor of this community as a role or as a job, but rather as doing life with like- minded people, helping each other to grow and serve Him. It has been an honour and a joy to lead this community and for that I thank them. I pray this book honours the journey we have been on together and inspires others to seek out what true community looks like this side of heaven.

Introduction

Planting the seeds deep within.

> *"God's seed is deep within them, making them who they are......As we keep His commands. We live deeply and surely in Him and He lives in us. And this is how we experience His deep and abiding presence in us, by the Spirit He gave us"*
> *(1 John 3: 9/23b-24: The Message).*

Have you ever wondered why many of our children don't grow to become deeply planted in Christ? One day I got some children to grow plants to teach the importance of having the right conditions for growth. I wanted to encourage them in their faith and experience the fruits of patience. The following week, when I went to look for the planters for the next lesson, I realised I had left them at the centre, locked up in a dark room. We might have planted the seeds correctly but a week without sun, water and nutrients was not a great start to the experiment.

I felt like a failure straight away. I thought, "I can't even do this for a plant, how am I going to do this for the children?" But, it helped me answer the initial question which is so often asked in ministry. With only a small amount of input, once a week, is it any wonder our children don't grow and become deeply planted in Christ. The plants did suffer and only a few grew, and when they did they were not healthy at all. They had tried so hard to look for light that their root system was very weak. When we think of a healthy plant, we think of deep roots; a strong foundation. We know that this, as well as food, sunlight and rich soil, all work towards a plant growing healthy and strong.

So, what is our role in this process?
A garden website said, "The moral? If you're going to plant a tree - be sure you plant it where it can grow."[1]

Are we creating environments where people can grow? Is there deep rich soil, full of nutrients and good things, where there is plenty of water and sun? We know the optimum environment for many plants to flourish; do we do the same in our churches, for our people? If that was the case, then the church would be overflowing with deeply strong Christians, attracting others to come and find the same deeply rich experience.

This book aims to unpack what that environment might look like.

> *the church is losing approximately 50% of its children during the years surrounding the transition they make to high school or to youth group*

It is not just one thing that is important, but rather a combination. It is a coming together of many things, a collision of elements that helps us to be deeply rooted in Him.

What will it take for us to be deeply and surely abiding in him so that we do not fall away? I know if we could answer this with 100% assurance we would follow it to the letter with our children and our ministries.

Yet I see so many of our children fall away. "In recent research done by Australian Children's pastor, David Goodwin, it showed that the church is losing approximately 50% of its children during the years surrounding the transition they make to high school or to youth group. Another observation was that children's ministry in most denominations did not give a lot of thought to long term faith development of the children, which could be a factor as to why many children leave church."[2]

"To get a healthy root system, plant them deep ....Your plant may not look nice at this time; but don't worry, in a few weeks it will grow and become much bigger. This procedure will promote rooting from the entire stem underground and will result in a plant with a robust root system."[3]

We all understand that to be deeply planted means to have a healthy root system. When I recently walked through the Australian bush, I was in awe of the majestic tress that had weathered the storms, the winds and the fires. Although they carried the marks of stress and pain, they were strong and

2   Goodwin David, 2013, *Lost in Transition or Not? - Addressing the problem of children leaving the church as they make the transition from childhood to youth.* Sydney Kidsreach
3   *www.gardening.about.com*

majestic to look at. It gave me a picture of what it means to abide in Him and to live deeply in Him. If we want this for our children we must do more than throw some teaching at them and hope for the best. There must be a better use of time and resources, with a higher percentage of positive outcomes. After all, we are talking about people's lives here.

We are losing too many children to continue to be careless about this principle.

I long for the children all around me to be deeply rooted in Christ; for Him to be their guide and teacher, that they might become more like Him. Maybe we are spending too much time and energy making sure they are deeply planted into a system or a program. Perhaps we have forgotten that being deeply implanted into Christ is the key.

Surely our focus should be on creating environments where children can become deeply rooted in Christ, rather than a leader, a group, or a ministry. To be deeply planted in Him means that wherever they go, or whatever happens, His truth and love for them doesn't change. That's true transformation isn't it?

In George Barna's book, *Revolutionary Parenting* we read that he worked hard at finding a sample of adults who fitted the criteria of believing the basic premise that "people are created primarily for spiritual purposes" [4] He found that 1 in 10 adults met these criteria. The parents had to meet the following standards:

Knowing, loving and serving God was a top priority.

Their faith in God was the highest importance.

They had to possess a Biblical worldview.

They believed that their main purpose in life was to love God with all their heart, mind and strength.

They currently had to be active in a vibrant community of faith.

Those who met the criteria were engaged in revolutionary parenting and defined success as intentionally facilitating faith-based transformation in

---

4   *www.barna.org/family-kids-articles, April 9, 2007*

the lives of their children. They made parenting a life priority. The research showed that the parenting approach determines whether children become devoted Christians[5]. This is a good start to helping our children become deeply rooted in Christ. It's how to get them to the place where "His love compels" (2 Corinthians 5:14), and they have no choice but to live for Him whatever the circumstances are. I want that for my children! I want that for the faith community I am committed to. I believe God desires that for us all.

Sometimes we have been guilty of focusing on just one thing; especially with children. We have concentrated on teaching them, without many of the other elements. That is like watering, watering, watering, without sun, good soil, nutrients, or an understanding of the conditions and where you place the plant. To simply continue watering, may just end in drowning the plant and, in the process, killing it.

Someone who is deeply rooted in Christ needs much more than we have been giving them.

"As we keep His commands we live deeply and surely in Him and He lives in us. And this is how we experience his deep and abiding presence in us, by the Spirit He gave us."
(1 John 3: 23b-24).

---

5   *www.barna.org/family-kids-articles, April 9, 2007*

Chapter 1

Creating environments where the generations can collide.

What does it mean to collide?

What does it mean to collide? The Collins[6] English Dictionary simply says: to conflict in attitude, opinion, or desire; clash; disagree; to crash together with a violent impact.

The word "collision" often has a negative connotation. To clash or disagree, is not a pleasant experience. People tend to spend a lot of time avoiding conflict. They don't want to experience a violent impact. The fact is, we collide whether we like it or not. What's worse is that the collisions are often within families, communities and even churches and often go without a positive outcome. Instead, they cause damage and go mostly unresolved. It is often easier to walk away, or simply clash and hurt each other, rather than work towards resolution that can then bring positive outcomes. Such positive outcomes normally will involve forgiveness, understanding, compromise and admitting wrong where appropriate. Too often families and churches become divided because of unresolved collisions and people never speak again.

You might say what a lovely way to start a book. This is going to be a hoot!

In this book, I would love to revise the word "collision". Let's look at how it might actually be a life transforming experience that creates environments for spiritual growth.

Let's look again at the definition of the word, "collide". In physics, collisions refer to the close approach of two or more particles or substances that result in an abrupt change of momentum or exchange of energy.[7]

Now that sounds better …even exciting! So, for this book, I want to focus on the positive ways that we can collide.

---

6   *Collins English Dictionary – Complete and Unabridged © HarperCollins Publishers 1991, 1994, 1998, 2000, 2003*

7   *http://www.thefreedictionary.com/collision*

> *"Truly intergenerational communities welcome children, emerging adults, recovering addicts, single adults, widows, single parents, teens whose parents are not around, the elderly, those in crisis, empty nesters and struggling parents of young children into a safe be challenging place to be formed into the image of Christ."*

Sure, when we collide it can be messy; it may feel uncontrollable, and will probably be painful and challenging.

But, it has the potential to transform us all. It has the potential to create an experience that you can't have on your own. That is not to say that these collisions are always going to be easy and comfortable. However, I do believe that they will be worthwhile and challenging, and even a catalyst for growth and change.

It is important to be able to define the word "generations". I understand that to "be intergenerational" is quite the buzz word today and therefore can be interpreted in different ways.

"Intergenerational" is generally understood as members of two or more different generations having some degree of mutual, influential relationship. This is best developed through cooperative interaction across the ages to achieve common goals.

"Truly intergenerational communities welcome children, emerging adults, recovering addicts, single adults, widows, single parents, teens whose parents are not around, the elderly, those in crisis, empty nesters and struggling parents of young children into a safe be challenging place to be formed into the image of Christ."[8]

When we talk about being truly intergenerational in this book it does not mean where several generations are in proximity with each other, but not necessarily engaged in meaningful relationships.

Intergenerational is a way of life. Making such a shift requires overcoming the individualistic mindset that is so strong in our culture and developing a community mentality in which all generations and ministry departments are valued and involved with each other in significant ways throughout the

---

8   *Allen, Holly C & Ross, Christine L, 2012, "Intergenerational Christian Formation", InterVaristy Press, USA, pg 63.*

church body. Cross-generational valuing must become an integral part of the congregation's collective story.[9]

When we combine two or more generations together within a created environment, the possibility of that "collision" can be transformational.

This book looks at how to create environments where the generations can collide, and to answer the following questions:

What could this positive experience look like?

Why is it valuable for people of all generations to "collide"?

What types of environments can be created that allow the generations to collide in such a way that it will be a transforming opportunity for all involved, and one that promotes spiritual growth?

I want to suggest five elements that are crucial to seeing this happen.

1. We must design environments to re-teach people how to play/be together.

2. We must breakdown "Silos" and aim for a holistic approach to our walk with Jesus.

3. We must empower with language to re-think effective ministry.

4. We must fight for true community; a community where there is acceptance, forgiveness, and unconditional love that is everyone's responsibility.

5. We must create a collaborative spirit, which helps everyone see the value of working together.

Let's expand the 5 key elements out.

We must design environments to re-teach people to play/be together.
My family often laugh at me when we are looking for a restaurant in which to eat. I will look in and see if I like the ambience or not. If I don't like

---

9   Snailum, Brenda 2010, *Promoting Intergenerational Youth Ministry Within Existing Evangelical Church Congregations: What Have We Learned?, Talbot Theological Seminary, Fall Issue.*

it, I won't want to go in. I am happy to move on. My husband will get frustrated because the food might be really good but we will never know, because I don't like the design or the feel of the place. That's the power of an environment! It reminds me of many churches. It doesn't matter what you are saying or serving, the environment, or lack thereof, can be a real barrier to certain non-believers and believers.

We run a camp every October. It has a reputation of being a very good camp. Of all the camps run at the campsite, it is known to be one of the most creative and visually stimulating ministry camps that we run. People will often say to me, "You go to a lot of trouble in the atmosphere you design. Surely it is not worth the effort for five days for a hundred and eighty children?"

Recently I received this random Facebook message:

Dear Tammy,

I have been trying to track you down for a number of years to thank you for running Minis Camps at Stanwell Tops. I became a Christian at one of your camps, "The Missing Piece" in 1990. I was a young country kid from Orange Church of Christ and Dave was my leader. I still remember some of the Bible studies and how you made the auditorium like the garden of Eden and then tore it all down over night after sin came into the world.

I have been helping lead kids Bible studies and youth groups for the last 15 years. I am currently working as an engineer in Perth Western Australia. My wife Sandy and I have just finished a series on "Covenant: How God keeps his Promise" for a teenage Bible study group at Redemption Church in Mt Claremont.

We trust and pray that God is continuing to use you

With love and fond memories from Western Australia,

Graeme White

remember that last time he had so much fun with his children. I know it is not always going to be that easy and, for these families in particular, it is not the complete answer to their problems but it was a great start.

More and more we need to realize that all ages need to learn to play together again. They need to learn to feel comfortable being together. I believe Jesus modelled this lifestyle and so should we as a Christian community. The ways to do this are endless. Throughout this book I will give many examples that I hope will spark your imagination to see that it is not a hard thing to do, and can be so transforming for all involved.

We must breakdown "Silos" and aim for a holistic approach to our walk with Jesus.

While I will expand on the concept of what it means to be "Siloed" in a later chapter, we must realize that much of what we do in church life can be very "Siloed". This means that a lot of the ministries are compartmentalized. They are divided up into smaller parts, in order to specialise in certain areas of ministry. It might be divided by age, hobbies, preferences of worship, or styles of presentations. While there is a place for compartments, they should not be to the exclusion of being all together.

It is important to create places where we can all come together and experience a "holistic" time together: spiritually, socially, physically, and intellectually. When we work together we have a better chance of colliding together in a way that can be transformational. A family must function holistically; to ignore parts of us is to be unbalanced. Today, in the Western world, the word "family" can be isolating as many people feel that society has defined family as two adults and two point five children.

But here is a better definition: A family is a grouping of individuals who are affecting each other intellectually, emotionally, spiritually, physically, psychologically.[11]

During a conversation with a non-Christian about the state of the world, and how we are in such a bad way, I said in frustration, "When is it all going to stop?"

---

11   *Schaeffer, E. 1975, What is a family?, Baker Book House, p. 170.*

His reply was, "When a group of people live in a way that is so authentic that people want to stop going down and start going back up!'

This is not only a great definition of what a Christian should be like, but how true community should show itself to the world.

In his book, *The Urban Halo,* Craig Greenfield tells of his call to go to Cambodia to help orphans of the poor. His original plan was to start an orphanage. He believed that taking the children out of the poverty situation and into a place with food and shelter, with other kids, would be the best way to help them.

After living in the slums with the people and doing a lot of praying and research he said, "Children thrived better in bad homes than in good institutions"[12]. As a result HALO was born, with the heart of helping communities and families to care for their own orphans. It is interesting that even in the poorest of communities there is still a strong pull toward caring and living all together. Even if that means struggling together, it is still often better than separation and segregation.

There is something very powerful we must learn from the developing world that we have lost. Craig Greenfield discovered in Cambodia that, because they all live so close and support each other, it was natural to care for each other's children. They may need help and support, but they were open to it. In this way he could say that children were better in bad homes than good institutions.

The issue I find very strong in Australia, is that we silo ourselves so much that we don't allow anyone to help, and we try to make out that we are all okay. But, behind closed doors there is trouble. If we truly understand the holistic approach, the way God designed it, we are not meant to do it alone. We are not meant to have all the answers and to be able to grow without outside help and support across the generations. Reggie Joiner and Carey Nieuwhof have recently released an excellent book, *Parenting beyond Your Capacity.*

> *They say that great parents realise we are not meant to do it alone; we need a community to raise a child*

---

12   Greenfield, Craig ,2007, *The Urban Halo, Authentic Publishing, p.72.*

They say that great parents realise we are not meant to do it alone; we need a community to raise a child[13].

The Biblical idea for the family is the whole family of God. So when we speak of being holistic, I am speaking of both the whole individual and the whole family of God. This book is about celebrating the belief that we can do more together than apart.

In Acts 2 we read of a time in the early church when the people ate together, shared possessions, sang, learned, prayed and were in each other's houses. It involved a lot of time together. At an "International Summit of Christian Camping" in 2012, there was much long-winded discussion and posturing among the representatives from many countries. They were discussing the issues of camping across the world and what changes needed to be made to be effective in Christian camping today.

After a series of long sessions my husband was sharing a meal with a delegate from Russia, who commented on how slow the program was progressing.

He said, "We will not solve these problems until we share much salt together".

My husband smiled, and realized yet again that in our Western world we want to do everything quickly and in a "siloed" manner. We don't realize that the power of many meals together is where we can truly create holistic community. It reminded me that we meet and have many intellectual conversations and thereby expect to change the world. But, that often only comes with creating true holistic community where we can meet physical needs, social needs and psychological and spiritual needs all at the same time.

There is another way to look at the holistic view as we approach our walk with Jesus. That is to understand that there are no age limits to the missional journey. We often segregate people into age brackets and limit what they can not only learn, but also what they can teach each other.

We all had a very powerful spiritual experience just recently when I was with my family. It was just as significant for me as it was for my nine year

---

13   Joiner, R.& Nieuwhof, C. 2010, *Parenting beyond your capacity*, David C Cook, USA

old, twelve year old and my husband, David. In fact it was more powerful because we shared it together, and saw it from all different perspectives.

It may be controversial to share this as I know there are many who feel strongly about climbing Uluru. But, our family did climb it and it was a very spiritual experience for us. When we arrived at the top of the rock, we all spent a bit of time quietly looking at the view, which is breathtaking. Wherever you looked it was stunning. We found a quiet place together, ate a sandwich and shared together what we were seeing. David, my husband, then shared his favourite psalm out of the Bible and we prayed together. There was a sense of being in – or more correctly, on – God's creation. The awe of His presence was real for us all. It is a moment we will never forget. There was no age limit there. We walked, ate, worshipped and marvelled together, and the age difference strengthened the experience. We all had different perspectives and were able to share them with each other. For Sam (our twelve year old boy), the sense of conquering God's amazing creation was exhilarating. He is a typical teenage boy. For Georgia (our nine year old girl), the sheer size of the rock overwhelmed her. David (my husband) shared his fear that he might have felt disappointed when he first saw the rock, but in fact it exceeded his expectations. It was a great connection with His father in Heaven. For me, everywhere I looked, it was different, new again, diverse, ever surprising. There were multiple joys everywhere I turned. It was again a reminder of the depth and diversity of God and His love for us.

It was all different, all good and transforming for us all at the same time, and age was not an issue. In fact it was a strength to share it holistically together.

So when we think about being holistic, we need to think not only about each of us personally experiencing God holistically across the physical, social, spiritual and emotional, but also across the generations. Different people's experiences and perspectives play a key role in helping us grow in our walk with Jesus.

We must empower with language in order to re-think effective ministry.
Language can be a barrier or a bridge to bring about change. If you think this is a petty thing, try an experiment for yourself. Take some time to

say a few words to a group of people and see what kind of response you get. For example the following words can evoke a positive or negative response:

> *"Don't be afraid to let your language change and evolve to reflect the world around you. Our language is as dynamic as our relationships are. Enjoy the movement."*

- Church
- Worship service
- Sunday school
- Family
- Christmas lunch
- Mothers' day / Fathers' Day

Depending on who you talk to, you will evoke a positive or negative response. The point is it is not so much about the words, but more about people's experience. Our memories or perceptions of something will evoke a response in us. It is not even about whether the response is true or not, but rather that the feelings are real and they can be a barrier or a bridge to bring about change. If our goal is to draw people to Christ, then surely we need to be aware that language can be positive or negative on that journey. It also helps us to confirm what we are about and what is most important to us.

The question is, do you want to be a barrier or a bridge to change? If you want to be a bridge to help people re-think effective ministry, then you need to understand the importance of language.

"Don't be afraid to let your language change and evolve to reflect the world around you. Our language is as dynamic as our relationships are. Enjoy the movement." [14]

For every ministry or group of people, language will be different and will need to be considered.

When we began a new community called "ICentral316", the core people who gathered came from a long tradition of church life. The greatest challenge was to embark on something that looked different from their past experiences. It was not that they didn't desire to do something new; it

---

14   Myers, J.R. 2007, *Organic Community,* Baker books, USA, p. 157.

was the fear of the unknown. There was a natural inclination to go back to what they knew because it was sometimes easier than breaking new ground.

Our people had a renewed understanding of the Israelites in the desert wanting so quickly to go back to Egypt. Even if it meant slavery, for some, it was better than the unknown. On that journey of re-thinking, language became a key for me as the leader, especially when sometimes they were unwilling or scared.

I was very deliberate about my language in order to help us all re-think what true community might look like.

As result, certain words have gone out of our conversation and have been replaced by others.

- Worship Service has been replaced by, Family celebration.
- Fellowship has been replaced by, Connect.
- Church has been replaced by, Community.
- Bible study has been replaced by, Life groups.
- Goals has been replaced by, DNA.
- The Board has been replaced by, the Leadership team.
- Senior Minister has been replaced by, Team Leader.

Words like Sunday school, Children's church and church service have gone completely out of our vocabulary. We are an "Intergenerational Creative Arts Community". The key words in our DNA that make us unique is that we are:

- Creative
- Accepting
- Transforming
- Intergenerational

I know that the thinking has changed for everybody. The language has been adopted. It helped us to re-think, restructure and know who we are. It helped us to be open to where God would lead us. That could not have happened unless we were deliberate in changing the way we spoke and using the new words to be a bridge to a new place rather than a barrier. It has released us as a community to stick to the goal: to grow closer to Christ, closer together, and to be a light to those around us who don't know Jesus.

Hugh Salter and Matt Smay describe their incarnation community like this: We are creating places of inclusive belonging where God's alternative Kingdom can be experienced.[15]

As they journey together, their language has been chosen deliberately to communicate and re-think the way they understand church.

"Words are powerful; take them seriously. Words can be your salvation. Words can also be your damnation"
(Matthew 12:37).

This journey will be different for each of you. The words will also be different. But, please understand that language will be a key barrier or bridge to whether people will be open to re-thinking in order to be effective in your community and ministry.

Hopefully you will see in this book that language and wording has been chosen very carefully to create bridges for people to change rather than trying to create barriers that stifle transformation.

We must fight for true community; a community where there is acceptance, forgiveness, and unconditional love that is everyone's responsibility.
What does it mean to fight for true community? I don't think we will ever experience it in the truest sense until we get to Heaven. However, I do think we are called to aim towards it anytime we can. (Matthew 6:9-11) You know when you get a glimpse of it. My response is always, "I want more of that".

In Acts 2 we read of the beginning of the Church. "All believers were together and had everything in common" (Acts 2: 44). We read in Acts that the people were in awe and saw many wonderful things, so much so that the Lord added to their number daily those who were being saved. When I read this passage I want to be in that community. It must have

15   Salter, Hugh and Smay, Matt 2008, *The Tangible Kingdom – Creating Incarnational community*, A Wiley Imprint, USA, p.xxi ,

been exciting times when the church was just beginning. They had unity and togetherness was celebrated. I am sure it was not all smooth sailing, but they knew they had to do it together. When we are together across the ages, we see community the way God designed.

All of us together with different giftings, different perspectives, varying life experiences, needing to display acceptance and tolerance, and desiring to feel a part of a bigger story.

We simply can't be a part of a true community on our own, or by continuing to only be with people of similar age, likes and dislikes.

"The church is the single, multiethnic family promised by the creator of God to Abraham. It was brought into being through Israel's Messiah, Jesus; it was called to bring transformative news of God's rescuing justice to the whole creation."[16]

1 John 2:6 says, "Whoever claims to live in Him must walk as Jesus did." When Jesus walked this earth, he was seen with people. He collided with all ages, all types of people, in all types of situations. People followed him where ever he went. Jesus created environments where truth could be experienced, lives could be changed, love could be shared and joy could be found.

In John 17, we read Jesus' final prayer for us. "The goal is for all of them to become one in heart and mind – just as you, Father, are in me and I in you. So they might be one in heart and mind with us. Then the world might believe that you, in fact, sent me."

Wow! His heart's desire for us, our mission and calling is all wrapped up in one sentence. It seems to me that when we work towards true community, we fulfil the great commission and find life to the full (John 10:10).

I think the hardest challenge of true community is that this requires a lot of compromise, acceptance of differences and forgiveness. It seems to me that we do all we can to eliminate anything that might cause situations where we have to do this. If things get hard or don't work out the way we want it, we simply remove ourselves from the situation. We see this in the

16   Wright, N.T. pg 200,, Simply Christian, Harper Collins, New York, .2006.

family, friendships, clubs, organizations and the church.

"But when generations collide, the ensuing conflict reminds everyone, Church is not just about me. Who knew that church could be the cure to narcissism?"[17]

Today, on Facebook, when you don't like something or you don't want someone to see something controversial, you simply "de-friend" them. You simply cut them off. We end up in isolation, in our own self-made silos. That way we don't have to deal with the hard conversations, accountability and even forgiveness. It is just too easy to do this in marriages, friendships and in Christian communities.

> *"But when generations collide, the ensuing conflict reminds everyone, Church is not just about me. Who knew that church could be the cure to narcissism?"*

For example, if certain people don't like a style of worship, we simply create a new style for them. If people don't like the style of the Christian community, ministers will say, "If you don't like us, just go down the road and you will find another that suits you."

While I do understand that sometimes it is about finding the right fit, there is also something important about loving and caring for the community that you have been given. It is not an easy conversation, or an easy thing to solve, but we must consider there are other options rather than simply leaving, and/or quitting, or worse "de-friending" when we don't like something.

Self-centeredness and age discrimination manifests itself in individuals within the church and can become a dominant force at work in generational cohorts and the culture at large. This deep-seated selfishness is a formidable foe that can potentially derail the best intergenerational ministry efforts. True intergenerational community is built on genuine love for every generation beyond a consumerist, "What's in it for me?", mindset.[18]

---

17   Hall, Chad, Fall 2006, "All in the family is now Grey's Anatomy: Today's Segregation Is by Age", "Leadership 27, pg 33

18   Snailum, Brenda 2010, Promoting Intergenerational Youth Ministry Within Existing Evangelical Church Congregations: What Have We Learned?, Talbot Theological Seminary, Fall Issue.

I spent some time with a beautiful family that had been connected to a Christian community for over twenty years. They gave everything to God, and to their Christian community, all through their childhood, teenage years and adulthood. As their children grew up, it became apparent that their children had learning disabilities and they were struggling to cope in the children's' ministries. They shared with me that ten months ago they left that church, because the ministry team were not prepared to work through how they would support their family, or minister to their children.

This is a family that understands their role in spiritually preparing their children, and was simply looking for the support of the extended Christian community on that journey. The saddest part for me is that they were sharing that in the past ten months, by not going to Church, they have grown closer together as a family and have been happier.

There is a growing issue with learning difficulties in local ministries. I realize there is no easy solution. But, my heart is heavy as I wonder, surely it is not the only solution, and surely it doesn't reflect acceptance and unconditional love? Why is it that this family felt as if the last ten months have been better not being connected to a community of believers. Ouch !

We must fight for true community and see that everyone plays a part in God's community. What are you doing to help build this in all ages, rather than eliminate or walk away when it doesn't suit us?

When I collide with God it changes the way I see the world.

When I collide with the world it changes the way I see God.

When I collide with others, I am not alone in the Journey.

We must create a collaborative spirit, which helps everyone see the value of working together.

We need to bring a collaborative spirit to the environment we seek to create, in order to see a positive collision.

To be collaborative is to be intentional, but with a lighter spirit. Have you ever been intentional about an event, or a party, or a holiday? Was there a time when, with all the best intentions, you wanted something specific to happen and it didn't?

I have had this many times. I remember a particular weekend trip with my family. We intentionally planned the time out, with the view that we really needed some quality time away. I remember when it all went sour and it is the worst time ever. I heard myself say to everyone, "We *will* have a great time together." But, it just didn't happen.

Then there are other times when we can plan a trip, and be very intentional about what we might do and how we might do it, and it turns out even better than we had planned. It becomes a key memory we all carry as very special.

So, what is this: pure chance? Pure luck? Sometimes you win, sometimes you lose?

We need to be careful with expectations when they become demands. We need to be careful about being intentional so that it doesn't become controlling and manipulative. That is when we must realize that with all the best intentions we cannot and must not control people.

So, when we think about creating a collaborative spirit, how is this key to helping create a positive collision?

The word, collaborate, speaks of joint effort rather than control. It is about empowering everyone in the process, while still being able to be intentional. It is about being open enough to move where the group goes together, even though the intention is still there to collide!

"The same is true for community. We can have some control over the environment in which community usually emerges, but we have little or no control over community actually emerging. We can intend for the process of community to begin, but we cannot create community intentionally."[19]

When my daughter, Georgia, was eleven years old, she had trouble sleeping. We learnt the hard way you simply cannot say, "Go to sleep", or tell her to just make the decision to go to sleep. In fact the harder you try to be intentional about sleeping, the harder it is to actually go to sleep. With the whole family, we created spaces and an environment where sleeping might be optimal. Yes, it was intentional, but with a collaborative spirit; realizing

---

19   *Myers, J.R. 2007, Organic Community, Green Press Initiative, USA, pg 127.*

that together we could help her. We were collaborative with the way we set up her room, the lighting and the way we spoke to her as she went to sleep. We decided it was okay that there were nights when she just couldn't sleep. We encouraged her to pray or read when she was up for hours not being able to sleep.

The collaborative part was important because she did not feel alone, and she needed us to be loving and positive. It simply was a different kind of intention, because I was without control. Yet together we could help her learn to put herself to sleep.

A collaborative spirit can go a long way to helping any collision become a positive one.

To summarise:

These five keys are not guarantees. I know today we all want "how tos": five sure-fire steps. When we collide there is no guarantee that it will always be positive and it certainly won't always be easy. However I know it can be life-changing, transformational and challenging.

Let's come back to the definition of collision: A brief dynamic event consisting of the close approach of two or more particles such as atoms, resulting in an abrupt change of momentum or exchange of energy.

There is no promise of "positive only" experiences, but a promise of change and growth. In my short forty four years of life I have learnt that it is often the painful collisions that produce the most growth in me, if I allow it to. I have also learnt that most good things take time. The sad fact is that this generation often runs away from any collision that takes time and effort and especially if it is a painful one.

"Spiritual progress is often made when one does not feel the increase, and one is strengthened while seeming to grow more infirm."[20]

---

20   *St Bonaventure, (1217-1274)*

I also want to state that while much of this book is about principles and keys that can be used in many settings, my passion is children and their families. Therefore, much of the discussions, ideas and examples will come from that perspective. The joy of the last eight years of ministry is that I found great comfort, depth and strength as we have gotten out of our silos and begun working across all ages and generations in our community.

There has been wisdom and growth right across the ages, which has been a wonderful environment for our kids and families to grow into. It has been a 'win-win' and one I am willing to shout from the mountain tops, until others see the great value of creating environments where the generations can collide.

We will explore more of why it is important to collide, even when it is a challenge, in the next chapter.

Time to Collide:

Think of the times where there has been a real connection for all of the people in involved in your community. What were some elements that were evident?

_____

_____

_____

What are the current environments you are creating in your faith community and what are they communicating to your people?

_____

_____

_____

Are there some environments that are causing "silos" amongst your people? What are some ways you can make some changes?

_____

_____

_____

When have you experienced true community? What was it about that experience that felt positive? Can you name important feelings and structures that helped create that true community?

_____

_____

_____

What are some words or language that put up barriers for your faith community, for your family, for the wider community? Why are the barriers there? How can you begin to break them down?

_____

_____

_____

Chapter 2

Why should we collide?

If you want to go fast – go alone; If you want to go far – go together.

(African Proverb)

We have talked about the fact that to collide is sometimes messy and challenging. I am also counting on the fact that you are reading this book because you have a passion, as I do, to see children and families grow deeper in Christ.

So why should we look at doing things differently? Can't we just tweak the things we are already doing and bring a little freshness to current programs? I have been speaking at children's conferences for over fifteen years now, and I see the value of creating an environment where workers can be refreshed. However, I am more concerned about the many that come to a day conference, go to the mountain top, get some new great idea, and when it doesn't work the way they have learned at the conference, they come crashing down in a heap. The ministry is hindered rather than refreshed!

Unfortunately many conferences today are still working on the "siloed" model. This is where a group of like-minded people sit in workshops together and download information. They never really have the space or opportunities to explore, and dream with each other or the speaker leading the workshop. It is mainly lecture-based with little interaction. Where is the collision in that? This is a formula that works in with people's time, finances and busy lifestyle. But the question remains, "Is it the best way to help bring about transformation in the lives of children and families?"

Many of the workshops are about improving your current environment, or adding the latest resource or idea. Now as a workshop speaker, I realise that God works in wonderful ways during these times. There can be an exchange of energy or change in momentum in this forum that can be very helpful to workers. I wouldn't be a part of this type of training if I didn't see the value in it. It also wouldn't be right if I was happy to simply do as we have always done, without questioning if we could be colliding in more effective ways.

Einstein says, "The definition of stupidity is to continue to do the same thing and expect a different result."[21]

I am not alone in seeing the need to collide, to do something different, and to re-think what we are doing to help this generation and their families grow deeper. Let's look at what others are saying.

Respected Christian voices

There are many Respected Christian Voices out there that speak strongly for the need for change, for something deeper, for collisions across the generations.

Churches need to understand their role in the collision process. "Churches alone do not, and cannot, have much influence on children. In fact the greatest influence a church may have in effecting children is by impacting their parents." [22]

Tim Elmore writes, "If we are going to connect with the Generation iY the following will be imperative:

Lay plans to mix the generations. Intentionally set times for adolescents to spend time with adults and younger children.

> *Einstein says, "The definition of stupidity is to continue to do the same thing and expect a different result."*

Teach practical life skills

Build in opportunities for service

Give plenty of opportunity to "practice" maturity.[23]

Joseph R. Meyers in his book, *Organic Community*, speaks of four descriptive patterns of belonging

---

21   http://www.brainyquote.com/quotes/authors/a/albert_einstein.html
22   Barna, pg Xvii.
23   Elmore, T. 2010, Generation iY – our last chance to save their future, Poet Gardener, USA. p.69.

that help us experience a deep sense of connection and community. The four patterns are Public, Social, Personal and Intimate. While he goes into great detail about each one and the role it plays, he makes it clear that, "We do not experience belonging in only one or two of these spaces. All four contribute to our health and connectedness. We need connections in all four"[24]

He speaks of the important role we play in ministry to "create environments and spaces that encourage the patterns of belonging and allow people to connect naturally in all kinds of ways." [25]

His final conclusion is that the "Primary responsibility of a church is to help people live whole, healthy lives. And as a part of the whole, the church could help people make healthy connections with those they encounter every day."[26]

Sister Joan D. Chittister, O.S.B., is a Benedictine nun, author and speaker. Sister Chittister holds a Master's Degree from the University of Notre Dame and a Ph.D. in Speech Communication Theory from Penn State University. She writes and speaks on women in the church and society; human rights and peace; justice in the areas of war and poverty, and religious life and spirituality. She is the founder of "Benetvision".

She speaks very powerfully and eloquently of the power of sharing across the generations:

Every elder in every community is a living history for the people to whom he or she will someday leave the earth to guide as good, as better, than they did in their own time but more important even than their knowledge is their ability; their call, to pass on stories to the later generations. Without the passing on of the stories, young ones are a group without character, without tradition, without the living memory of how and why they came together in the first place. Family tales have always been the parables one generation handed down to the next to tell us who we are and where we came from when the young realise what may be lost forever if the next generation does not take responsibility for maintaining it.

---

24   *Meyers, pg 45*
25   *Meyers, pg 49*
26   *Meyers, pg 166*

Reggie Joiner in his brilliant book, *Think Orange*, says, "What we should be really concerned about is our collective ability to influence a generation to have a stronger and deeper and more authentic relationship with God. The church and home are critical platforms for that mission, but both are losing ground: both entities are struggling to be effective." [27]

Reggie Joiner is not just talking about adding a new program to your church for families. He is talking about re-thinking the way we have done things. We need to evaluate what we do and create new ways to influence those to whom we minister. His thinking has been a key catalyst for me to re-think how we collide with the generations to bring about a more holistic approach to ministry in new ways for this generation.

Mike Yaconelli wrote passionately in a web article about how to minister successfully to youth, claiming that the most effective way was to "be church".

"Somehow, being with a group of diverse people week after week caused a bond to be formed... Community isn't complicated. It's just a group of people who grow old together. They stick with each other through the teenage years, marriage, children, getting old, sick, and family dying – all the while teaching each other how to follow Christ through the rugged terrain of life."[28]

In a recent article, *Intergenerational Ministry beyond the Rhetoric*, from Fuller Youth Institute, Snailum and Griffin made the following observation. "Intergenerational is a way of life. Making such a shift requires overcoming the individualistic mindset that is so strong in our culture, and developing a community mentality in which all generations and ministry departments are valued and involved with each other in significant ways throughout the church body.. As one panellist shared, "The vision of the church needs to include assimilating our children and youth into the church today, not some day."[29]

How open are you to re-think? How open are you to Collide?

---

27   Joiner, R. 2009, *Think Orange*, David C. Cook, USA, p.80.
28   Yaconelli, M. 2002, A better idea that youth ministry http:/wpcstudents.org. CCM Communications Leadership/Leadership tools/growth articles.
29   Griffin, April, 2011,*Intergenerational Ministry beyond the Rhetoric*, from Fuller Youth Institute.

So... Why do you Collide?

1. Parents need to be reminded of their role with their children
"The spiritual nurture of children is supposed to take place in the home. Organizations and people from outside the home might support those efforts, but the responsibility is squarely laid at the feet of the family."[30]

Ivy Beckworth says, "The churches' ministry to children is broken… when we depend on our programs and curriculum to introduce our children to God – not our families and communities….and perhaps most importantly, it's broken when the church tells parents that its programs can spiritually nurture their children better than they can."[31]

Michelle Anthony in her book *Spiritual Parenting* says, "I want to parent the child or children that God gave me in such a way that I first honour God, and then second, create the best environment to put my children on the path of the divine". [32]

Ms Anthony outlines ten environments for children to flourish in and clearly states that, "Our goal as parents should be to endeavour to pass down our faith to the next generation in such a way that they will be able to pass down their faith to the following generation in our absence… and all that will remain is that which is transferred successfully to our children, and our children's children, so that faith will endure to all generations"[33]

2. We need to understand the need for the greater community to be a part of the faith process for a child.
"The faith of children is most likely to grow when they have the opportunity to associate with adults who are growing persons who know and love God. The child's faith is inspired when he or she belongs to an inclusive community that seeks to live out God's love" [34]

"Most of us can look back over spiritual journeys and recall people who had a positive spiritual impact on us; teachers, coaches, neighbours, bosses, church leaders, or friends. Looking back, we'd probably conclude that God

---

30   Barna, p.12.
31   Beckworth, I. 2004, Postmodern Children's ministry – Ministry to children in the 21st Century, Zondervan, p.13-14.
32   Anthony, Michelle,2010, Spiritual Parenting, David C Cook,, p.12.
33   Anthony, pg 26
34   28 Stonehouse, Catherine 1998, Joining children on the spiritual journey, Baker Academic, Grand Rapids, MI; p.37.

> *The fact is that even eating together at the dinner table for a meal each day is a rarity in many houses*

used human relationships to grow us closer to Him. When church leaders elevate community and groups–based ministry, we give people a chance to form significant relationships that can help them grow closer to God." [35]

Joel B. Green says, "Generations of children who are provided with less and less contact with faithful agents of Christian mission, fewer and fewer models of relationship-building, and so for whom faith becomes so personalised that it need not even find expression within one's own family"[36]

3. Current trends show there is a deep need to collide across the generations.

This current generation in Western Society has seen the "creation of silos".

Homes

We can find ourselves in siloed environments even in our home, with our own rooms, computers and TVs. It is not hard to be in the same house and yet spend a night not communicating to the people you live with. For many families a night together is watching their favourite TV show. The fact is that even eating together at the dinner table for a meal each day is a rarity in many houses. That is especially true if you insist that the TV isn't on while you are trying to eat a meal together.

I spoke to a distressed parent recently who was scared to go into her fifteen year old son's room and ask him to stop playing his internet game to come and eat with the family. She said she was literally afraid he would beat her up. Now I know there are many more issues going on there to cause this extreme case, but the isolation in that family is affecting everyone and everything.

Public

In public the way we use smart phones can silo us from face to face conversation. While we were on holidays with another family, I was amazed

35   *Joiner, R 2009, Think Orange, , David C. Cook, USA , Concentrate 9.5*
36   *Green, J, 2008, Tell me a story: The Child of the Bible – perspectives on Children from the Acts of the Apostles, Grand Rapids, Mich. : William B. Eerdmans Pub., p. 229 .*

to see that when we sat on a train, bus or in a car the other family would all pull out their iPhones and go into their own little worlds. There would be no conversation.

In contrast my children, husband and I would be looking out at the snowy capped mountains and talking about the beautiful views and what we were going to see that day. I was mocked when I made the comment about the lack of conversation with the other family, because the iPhone is a status symbol not to be messed with. My children, of course, were very envious of them, and would jump at any chance they could get to play with the phone. It is so accessible and exhaustive in possibilities. I understand the temptation to go there and escape the real world, or to multi-task. We all love the feeling of being connected at all times. I understand that pull, but I am concerned about the addiction it is creating in our world today if we are not able to have personal self control. There is a fear of the isolation even within a crowd of people.

I have been to Conferences, where some of the opening statements suggested that if you weren't on twitter and able to twitter during the speakers you were missing out on an important aspect of the conference. There I was, concerned that my phone was on silent so it didn't interrupt the speaker, and they were saying, "Please twitter throughout".

That meant that many people in the audience had their heads down concentrating on their phone most of the time the speaker was speaking. I do a lot of speaking and I really struggle with that concept. I may be showing my age, but I find it a really isolating thing speaking to someone who is not looking at me. In fact I was always taught that in public speaking you can't connect with people if you don't give them eye contact. Now as speakers we are battling the desire to communicate and connect with people who just won't look at you because they will be on computers or iPads or phones for the majority of the time. I am over having conversations with people while they are texting and looking at their phone. The conversation must be had about appropriate boundaries and balance; for when we do and don't utilize technology. Children in particular find it very difficult to self-monitor healthy boundaries in this area and they need good examples around them.

Church Life

The normal scenario for Western church life is to walk in on a Sunday morning; check your children into the children's program, babies into the nursery, youth in at the youth program and adults in the main sanctuary. Large churches will often have a safety policy where anyone not authorised cannot enter a room with children or babies without permission. If a baby cries a number goes up on the wall so the parent must go and get the baby so it doesn't disturb the adult church experience for others. We are all in our own specialized rooms, often passively listening to God's teaching. For the majority this is the one and only experience of God's presence in their week.

Church in our current format is very new in Christendom, about two hundred years old at the most. Sometimes we need to step out of our cocoon and check if it is what God intended when He asked us to be the light of the world. In the current silo situations, I am not even sure we are being a light to each other.

Of course there is a valid place where different age groupings, gifting and levels of learning find value in being together. But, if it becomes the only means by which we grow and worship God then I believe we are missing the core understanding of what God meant about "Koinonia", community.

To collide together in community means we need to explore the concept that there is much more we can do together as a worshiping, loving community than we think, or have been led to believe.

School

Even in the schooling system we have compartmentalised and specialised to the degree that we are missing out on some key factors that prepare us for real life.

Dr Mel Levine writes, "Years of schooling and parenting have entirely missed the elusive target: work-life readiness. Our graduates may well lack the practical skills, the habits, the behaviours, the real world insights, the frames of mind pivotal for career start-up. Their parents and teachers have unwittingly let them down. Adulthood has ambushed them" [37]

> *This is the first generation that does not need leaders to gain information. Information largely comes from peers*

Age grading first happened in the 1920s and many would suggest that this has not been all positive. By the 1930s, as High Schools became compulsory, more and more teens lost emotional ties with other adults and parents and began defining themselves by other students, not adult role models. While almost everyone agrees with a good education, like all things there are trade-offs. Isolating children and youth into their own age groups is one of them. It is interesting to note that this occurred not that long ago.

In our son's school, they specialise in the creative arts. While that sounds as though I am contradicting myself, our son came home so excited because they had made multiple drama companies within the school. They were comprised of students from all the years. Sam found himself in a drama company with students from Year 7 through to Year 12. He loved interacting with the year 11 and 12 students and learning from them. He found it very inspiring. It made sense to me and it was very refreshing to hear the school was doing that.

Of course the whole buddy system in schools has been a huge success and now, in our daughter's school, they have strategically structured social groupings where the sixth grade students lead the discussion and representatives from all years are a part of it. These are small glimpses of positive change and it is great to see teachers realising that there is much to be gained across the ages if the right environments are created.

World of Technology

Social networking takes our young people to a place where most of their interaction is through a screen. This is the first generation that does not need leaders to gain information. Information largely comes from peers. They lack the wisdom from other age groups to help them grow to adulthood. "As a result, many don't learn how to interface with folks from a different

---

37   Levine, Mel 2005, *Ready or Not Here Life Comes*, Simon and Schuster, New York, pg 5.

generation. Life for them is like an isolated compartment containing mostly people just like them." [38]

This again is not only an issue for children. All too often we have successfully silenced the elderly as not worth listening to. Our focus is on managing their old age. We have lost all respect for grandparents, unless they can babysit our children. The isolation for the elderly is that they cannot often speak the internet/twitter/iPhone language and so we disregard their views and thoughts.

The social networking world can be so isolating that many people re-create themselves and can almost live, get married and be absorbed into a virtual world they have created for themselves. In this world they can be anything they want to be, and no-one else need know about it….or so they think? I have been amazed at the things people will say on Facebook, that I know they would not say to my face. It is as if they are two different people. The ultimate isolation would be to actually be two or three different people, and if you are clever no-one needs to know.

Mark Bauerlein says, "Young people have never been so intensely mindful of and present to one another, so enabled in adolescent contact. This contact wraps them up in a generational cocoon reaching all the way into their bedrooms. The autonomy has a cost. The more they attend to themselves, the less they remember the past and envision a future." [39]

It begs the question: How can this generation grow into healthy adults unless we help them break out of their cocoons and help them collide with the other generations?

The computer world is not just an issue for our children and young people. Studies show that parents are just as dependent on technology as their children. Parents are using technology and media to nearly the same degree as their eleven-seventeen year olds and many feel it has been a positive influence on their families. Most feel unconcerned about it and think it is neither good nor bad.

---

38   Elmore, p.45.
39   Bauerlein, Mark, 2008, The dumbest generation: how the digital age Stupefies young Americans and jeopardizes our future, Penguin, New York, p10.

The question is whether families are in control of their technology or being controlled by it. This usually shows itself when technology has been cut off. The kind of reaction you get makes it evident who is in control.

I need to state clearly, that I believe technology has given us a lot and there is so much to celebrate and enjoy, but like anything good there must be boundaries and balance.

It is not the technology that is the problem, it is the user. Research backs up that "technology seems to amplify the relational patterns and problems already in place: families that have healthy and frequent conversations find technology aiding that process, while families without such healthy interactions find that technology exacerbates the isolation of its members."[40]

4. Instantaneous gratification

Today everything is instant and bite-sized. We get frustrated if something doesn't happen instantaneously. We have McJobs, McMarriages, McCommitments... Our children today are growing up with four or five dads that maybe hang around for three to five years. Young people today are leaving school with the expectation that they will probably have ten or so careers in their lifetime, because that is normal. They will happily leave a job they have started because of the way they are treated, or if it gets too hard, or if they are bored. It is simply too easy to quit. Like a video game, they look for the cheats. It is part of the rules; a way to get around the hard parts and move on.

The fact is that, wherever we are and whatever we are doing, with a Smart phone we can simply use Google and get the answers instantaneously. It is an incredibly powerful and useful tool in our hands, but it will not come without consequences for the generation that has only known this as the answer to every problem.

It is scary how easily we believe everything Google tells us, and yet this younger generation is constantly questioning God and even older wiser voices more and more.

---

40   *Barna, George September 2011, "How technology is influencing families," www.barna.org/ family-kids-articles.*

A recent study of high school students who used their mobile phones more than ninety times a day discovered that the most common reason given was that they were unhappy and bored. They also found that these teens were also significantly more depressed and anxious than their peers who used their phones fewer than seventy times a day[41].

This next generation is longing for the instantaneous gratification they get from sending texts constantly, but in fact there are far more frightening side effects from their actions such as, Anhedonia (explained later in the text), depression and anxiety that we must as parents and adults help them get back into control.

I fear for the lack of problem-solving skills in our young people today. I see them giving up so easily when things get too tough. To encourage them to stick with things and persevere is to go against the grain of their peers and the world they live in. It is an uphill battle that I will not quit, but I admit it is not easy. This generation seems to be looking for the easy way out of most things and I fear the baby busters have not helped, as I listen to my peers constantly trying to work out how they can retire and not ever work again.

In the light of this issue the collision with wisdom that has been around before Google, needs to be reinstated as valuable and worth listening to. It will not happen overnight, it is not an instantaneous fix, which is why it is being overlooked as a viable option for our young people.

5. Overwhelmed by current lifestyle

Generation Y is simply overwhelmed. The transition from childhood to adulthood can lead to stress that is overwhelming. In 2007, the American College Health Association surveyed college students and 94% reported feeling overwhelmed by their lifestyles.[42]

The Australian Childhood foundation conducted an online survey in 2007. They found that:

> 51% of children felt unwelcome in shops and cafes.

> 88% believed companies tried to sell them things they don't need.

---

41   Hart, A. 2007, *Thrilled to Death*, Thomas Nelson, p.77.
42   *National college Health Assessment Spring 2007, reference group data report 55, No 4 (Jan-Feb 2007): p.195-206.*

36% believed that adults don't really care what they think.

57% were worried about what others thought about them.

40% said they don't ever feel like they are doing well.

Children need adults to help them interpret their world. They need adults to help with the pressures and pace of modern life

The authors concluded, "Children need adults to help them interpret their world. They need adults to help with the pressures and pace of modern life."[43]

This is not simply an issue for children; we are seeing it right across the generations. If adults are feeling overwhelmed, then of course we are modelling this to our children and young people. The pressure to succeed, do well at school, even to be rich and famous seems to be at the forefront of adult's and children's thinking. The pressure of it all is overwhelming. I have watched a group of committed adult Christians in my own community go from being committed to meeting together and connecting together on a weekly basis six years ago, to now, where (although the desire is still there and very strong), it is a rare week when we all get together. The current lifestyle overwhelms us all so that even a weekly commitment to pray, learn, and listen to each other is a challenge.

What does that say to our children?

The pressure of succeeding at school is overwhelming. I have ached as I have mentored children from nine years of age. For years I see their commitment and passion grow along with a strong desire to serve God, until they go into year 12. This is the final year of High School in Australia. It consumes them and then often the social world takes over and they walk away from God and all that they have claimed to be important. I even see some parents encouraging this move as it seems the exam results, getting a job, and having a social life is so much more important than walking with God. I do understand that education, work and social life are important, but I ache when I see God get our scraps. The saddest part of all is that I don't see these young people being really happy. They are stressed and consumed with the lifestyle they have thrown themselves into.

---

43   *Australian Childhood Foundation, Children's fears, hopes and Heroes Survey, 2007*

These effects have resulted in the government crying out for someone to help the families of Australia. In the news just recently there has been an outcry from Sydney University Professor, Patrick Parkinson, pleading with the government to set up charitable trusts in each council to support marriages and families through relationship counselling and child rearing education in order for the community to take responsibility for repairing the damage.

The latest report, *For Kids' Sake*, shows that children's wellbeing has deteriorated in the past ten to fifteen years. It shows that self-harm for children aged ten to fourteen has increased by 66% and by 90% for girls aged fifteen to seventeen years. The number of children who reach the age of fifteen without an intact family and without both their biological parents together has almost doubled. Researchers believe that family breakdown has played a significant role and are doing all they can to strengthen marriages and family to stay together.[44]

"How we support marriage then, as the protective institution of family, particularly the welfare of children, is of profound importance." [45]

It is getting interesting when the government is calling for families to stay together. God's design of a safe environment to grow up in is being significantly weakened.

For Kids sake – Repairing the social environment for Australian Children and Young people, A paper prepared by Professor Patrick Parkinson AM, University of Sydney, had some very insightful recommendations that have been put to Federal Government in 2011. The lengthy document recommends among other things:

1. The encouragement of various community groups, including church and welfare, to offer relationship training programs free for their communities.

2. Programs that deal with parent-child relationships must focus on the importance of healthy relationships between parents, for the health and welfare of the children.

44   *Do more to protect kids: Christian Lobby, ninemsn.com.au/article, September, 2011*
45   *Kevin Andrews, families spokesperson, Canberra, www.theaustralian.com.au, Sept, 2011*

3.   The need for, and importance of, more programs which will support parents emotionally, psychologically and practically, to reduce the risk of child abuse and neglect, and to lessen the degree of isolation.

We are being bombarded by images, ideas and points of view. I hear adults and children saying all the time, "Where is God, I don't see Him anywhere? But my response is, "Where can He fit in?"

It is very difficult to find places of solitude now that the internet, computers, phones, and iPads etc are so portable and never leave our side. While I was driving the other day my phone rang and our son was agitated because I didn't answer it. He said, "Mum, don't you know it is rude not to answer your phone?" I explained that I was driving and it is illegal and dangerous to answer the phone at that time.

Then I began a discussion to stress how it is not rude to not answer the phone as it is actually intruding into my world and expecting me to drop what I am doing to answer it. Our teenager did not see it that way. To get a call, to be texted, or twittered is a way to feel accepted and valued. Any spare minute we have we fill it with messages, games, YouTube, or Angry Birds. There are "apps" on phones and their only purpose is to simply numb the mind and allow for no time where there could be silence. Where can God break in? Where can reflection happen?

When we walk, drive, sit on a plane, sit on a train, or sit in a restaurant we can have music playing in our ears, while we're surfing the net and texting a friend. We wonder why we can't turn off at night; why we are overstimulated and overtired.

It is the biggest depleter of children's pleasure. Dr Joan Luby of Washington University School of Medicine in St Louis, believes the "most specific symptom of depression disorders in kids under the age of six is something called "Anhedonia – essentially, appearing not to have fun while at play"[46]

Arch Hart would say that Anhedonia is a growing concern in the Western World today. It is the overstimulation of adrenalin, which leaves us overwhelmed and depressed. "Children who are overscheduled with

46   Jim Dryden, "Depression in Preschoolers", Washington University in St Louis News & Information, http:/mednews.wustl.edu/tips/page/normal/4172.html

structured activities are missing the chance they have to dream, to fantasize, to make their own world work the way they want it." [47]

How will we handle the quiet places or time to truly reflect on our lives? What would happen if we collided with actual people face to face?

6. "Cotton Wool Kids"

We have overprotected our children and young people so much that we have not prepared them for adulthood. When I was a child, my favourite part of a camp was to go into the dark at night and play spotlight. We couldn't see a thing, we got bumped and fell over, we laughed and we were proud of our bruises. Today when I try to play spotlight with children, they cry and say it is too scary and too hard and we often have to end the game early. We have bathed them with safety belts, safety policies, safety everything. This has stopped us from doing most of the things I would want to do with youth today in order to push their limits and stretch them.

"As parents, we don't want them out of our sight. As educators, we're concerned about liability and feel we need to avoid risk. We believe we are protecting our future by protecting them. In reality, we may be harming the future." [48]

The media and parents have so "loved" this generation. Our children have been told by Hannah Montana and many others that they can have the "best of both worlds". As a result they are the most narcissistic generation in History. [49]

"Neighbourhood play is a thing of the past and lock-down homes are children's primary playground" [50]

This speaks to the duty of care, a growing trend that is found right across all work with children, which is important. But my suggestion would be that instead of wrapping them in cotton wool, we need to work hard at creating safe environments where relationships are known and strong. It is a growing issue with the mega-church structures where children can be mistaken for a number to be signed in and out.

47	*Hart, p.95*
48	*Elmore, p.22.*
49	*Twenge, Jean M. and Campbell, K. 2009, The Narrcissim Epidemic: living in the age of Entitlement. Free Press, New York.*
50	*Yount Jones, Christine 2009, Executive Editor of Children's Ministry.com.*

We have been guilty of covering them in cotton wool out of love for them, but in the end we are not preparing them for real life. I will often say to my own children, "The sooner you work out that life is hard the better you are going to be", and I have been ridiculed for that. But I fear for the prince and princess world that so many of the children I work with live in, and how they are ever going to cope when confronted by the realities of life.

Recently I was at a Cross Country carnival with our youngest child. She hates running and wanted to quit. I explained to her that there will always be things we don't like to do, and that running was one of these to her. I suggested it was a good chance to have a nice walk with friends and an opportunity for some fitness. I explained, "You don't have to be the best, but you can do your best and make the best of the situation".

Of course the competitive spirit on the day is always there, and there are some great runners, for whom running is their thing. May I add that this process was very difficult for me as throughout my childhood I was a state cross-country runner, and very competitive, so it took all of me not to push her to "go for it". She did ask me to prepare her for the run as her friends were all getting serious about it. I tried hard not to become one of those pushy mums. I simply encouraged her to cheer those girls on, but not to feel pressured. I told her, "If you push yourself too much you will do something silly. Pace yourself and do your best. That is all that is required."

One little girl, I call the "princess" of the group, turned up in a full running suit and so did her mother! They were colour-coordinated and looked great together. They looked the part, but I happened to know that she was not a runner. Parents beside me were all commenting about how great they both looked and how good they must be. Our daughter Georgia started to panic and I said, "Just run your race, honey. I am proud of you".

Well off they went, and eventually 1st, 2nd, 3rd came back…then everyone else staggered in slowly. The parents around me were all waiting and surprised that the little girl with all the cool running gear hadn't come in yet. Georgia came in 2nd last, but she sprinted to the end. I had tears in my eyes as I was so proud that she finished something she hated. She had persevered to the end. The judges were getting worried as one girl was missing. Sure enough the "princess" in all the right gear had quit halfway through. Her mum had picked her up and brought her back to their bags. They were sitting having a drink and a snack and hadn't told anyone.

I have got to ask, what are we preparing our kids for when we treat them like protected princesses? As parents, we have to consider whether we are preparing our children for the real world.

As we have aimed to create environments where the generations can collide in our local church community, the strongest push back has been the parents who don't want to hang out with their own children. They would rather someone else do it, while they go and do adult stuff. This is seen right across the spectrum, from those on the poverty line who live in abusive situations, as well as the very rich, who are too busy with their lifestyle and commitments.

These "cotton-wool-kids" really do desire to change the world; they just don't have what it takes to accomplish their lofty dreams. When the work becomes difficult, they change their minds and move on to something else. "The new term for them is "Slactivists" – they are both slackers and activists. Consequently, for most of them, their involvement in causes is limited to buying a "Live Strong" wristband or signing a petition on a website." [51]

When we become overprotected, there are aspects of our character that don't get developed. The major fear I have is that we are debilitating our kids for the future. When we do not teach them endurance we stop them from learning that it is worthwhile to stay committed to a goal and to complete a task. If we do not teach them empathy, they will not learn how to see and feel what others do. If we don't teach them responsibility, they will not learn to do what is right, especially when they are acting alone. When we don't let them venture into new and challenging situations they don't learn to communicate and connect with people who are not like them. When we don't teach them patience we don't give them the opportunity to experience the greater reward that comes with waiting. To do this we need to create collision experiences with others. There is valuable life lessons that cannot be learned when wrapped up in cotton wool and in isolation.

The cyber world idea of a good friend is the number of friends you have on Facebook. This is a protected place where you sit in your own comfort and

---

51   Elmore, p.27.

accept friends that you may not even know. This concept of friendship may be safe, but it does not help children learn conflict resolution, listening skills or determination etc. Of course cyber bullying is very real and emotionally scarring. It is a growing issue, but once again it is largely a result of the lack of personal maturity that our children have developed as they are growing. They find themselves in a world they have not been prepared for, because they have been overprotected.

7. Longing to learn differently

The current trends show that if we are going to reach this generation we need to be willing to do things differently. While it may seem that much of the above discussion has been negative about the state of our nation, I do not believe all is lost. But future collisions will need to look different from what we have rolled out over the past forty years.

Children learn best by doing, using their senses, and exploring the world around them. It's how God designed them. Given the choice (and choice is the key) to watch someone else do something or experience it themselves, today's children will opt for the latter. Experience is the new frontier and we must join children on the adventure."[52]

If we are going to reach our children and the iY generation with the message of Christ, we need to understand it is going to have to come in a different format than the one we have grown up with. This is harder still for the "boomer" and "builders" who are two generations removed. But the sad thing is that many young people have grown up

There is valuable life lessons that cannot be learned when wrapped up in cotton wool and in isolation

feeling that the older generations have nothing to offer them. While we need to appreciate that we need to do things differently, it is also vital to understand that this does not happen without the other generations. We all play a key role in the collision process and we all benefit from it as well.

Tim Elmore says that to connect with this culturally potent group, adults need to observe that they want to belong before they believe.

---

52   *Anderson, Patty 2009, senior product developer for Groups Children's ministry Essentials, Group Publishing.*

They want to experience before an explanation.

They want a cause before they want a course.

They want a guide on the side before they want a sage on the stage.

They want to play before they pay.

They want to use but not be used by others.

They want a transformation, not merely a touch.

All this stresses that we need to do it differently and we need to do it together. It requires a sometimes physical, often emotional, and always spiritual collision of sorts to be able to be effective.

Time to Collide:

Take some time out to consider the following questions in your own context:

1. What is something new that you have read in this chapter that has challenged you to think more seriously about colliding?

_____

_____

_____

_____

_____

2. What is one change you can make in your ministry that can help break down the silos in our family, churches, school, and computer world or in public?

_____

_____

_____

_____

_____

Chapter 3

We have a biblical mandate to collide

Eugene Peterson, translator of the popular Biblical paraphrase *The Message*, writes this: "Every generation faces a changed culture, different social problems and challenges, new patterns of work, evolving economic and political conditions. Much of what a Christian community in each generation does is learn together how this is done in its particular circumstances."[53]

I believe we have a Biblical mandate to consider what it means to create environments where the generations can collide. Let us look at what the Bible says.

Parents need to collide with their children

"I'm chewing on the morsel of a proverb;
I'll let you in on the sweet old truths, Stories we heard from our
fathers,
Counsel we learned at our mother's knee.
We're not keeping this to ourselves,
We're passing it along to the next generation – God's fame and
fortune
The marvellous things he has done
He planted a witness in Jacob, set his word firmly in Israel
Then commanded our parents to teach it to their children
So the next generation would know, and all the generations to come
Know the truth and tell the stories so their children can trust in God
(Ps 78: 2-7; The Message)."

---

53   *Is Fryling the author? Then it should be set out as: Fryling, Robert A. 2010, The Leadership Ellipse: Shaping how we lead by who we are, Inter-Varsity Press, p.13. If Peterson is the author then put Peterson, Eugene instead of Fryling etc.*

God is at work telling a story of restoration and redemption through your family. Never buy into the myth that you need to become the "right" kind of parent before God can use you in your children's lives

God always intended for his truth and promises to be shared through relationships, from generation to generation. Yes, there is a place for formal instruction, but the power of a loving relationship with Jesus is best caught not taught. There is no doubt the most powerful place of influence is in the family unit. It is here that life commandments are taught whether you are strategic or not.

To be strategic in this context is to make it priority, or to be collaborative in planning key events where the family can collide. Family bonds and ties are strong. There is power when the truths of God are carried from generation to generation, both by stories and by the way we live as parents.

Every parent knows that their children mimic them even in the smallest of ways. Just when you think they are not watching, they are. They learn by living with us. The challenge is, what story are we telling? There is no point in saying education is important, if we don't teach that by our lives. There is no point in saying healthy living is important if we don't tell that story by our own living and words. The same is true about the place of God in our lives. Sending our children to church, or kids' club, or helping them connect in with a good, older, Christian role model is only half the battle. They are looking to see what our life story tells them. Nine times out of ten that is what they will come to believe for themselves.

What stories are we telling our children?

"God is at work telling a story of restoration and redemption through your family. Never buy into the myth that you need to become the "right" kind of parent before God can use you in your children's lives. Instead, learn to cooperate with whatever God desires to do in your heart today so your children will have a front-row seat to the grace and goodness of God."[54]

Children need to collide with grandparents

"Read up on what happened before you were born: Dig into the

---

54   *Joiner, p.48.*

past, understand your roots. Ask your parents what it was like be-
fore you were born; Ask the old-ones, they'll tell you a thing or two
(Deuteronomy 32:7; The Message)."

When our son started High School, his school was right next to my father's workplace. I asked Dad if he could take Sam to school each day. Every morning he picked him up at 7.45 am and they had a fifteen minute drive to school, five days a week.

Over the years I've lost count of the amount of times I have heard Sam say, "You know Poppy says…". We never realised at the time the significance of that car trip as Sam was starting High School, and going into a difficult time of teenage change. He suddenly had this connection with Poppy every morning as he started each day. It may have been just a short story, or a quick conversation, but Sam listened to so much more than we ever realised. I am not even sure my dad realises, but it was an important collision. It was a perspective that David and I couldn't give him, because of our age and stage in life.

Children need grandparents in so many ways: as continuity with the past; as a comfort, and a feeling of the specialness of being with their father's father or mother's mother. There is a security in having a grandparent say, "I used to do this with your mother".[55]

Youth need to collide with Children

"There should be no division in the body, but that its parts
should have equal concern for each other
(I Corinthians 12:25; ESV)."

A young person came into our midst and began to lead our youth. She is an amazing young lady and I am doubly blessed as she has taken a shine to my daughter. Georgia just adores her and talks about her as the big sister she never had. They hang out in the afternoons. She picks Georgia up and they go for walks down the beach.

Georgia had been struggling with sleep anxiety and this young woman went through a similar thing when she was young. So they talked about

---

55   Schaeffer, E. 1975, What is a family?, Baker House books, p.158.

that and she was very supportive of her. This relationship is very special and valuable. Any parent wants to have someone speaking positively into their child's life. They might say the things we would like to say but, seemingly, it sounds better when it comes from an adored big sister.

"Every son and daughter needs other adult voices in their lives who will say things a Christian parent would say... One of the smartest things mums and dads can do is to participate in a ministry where they can find the right kind of adult influences for their kids."[56]

We need to be praying and looking for ways for the youth to collide more and more with the children in our communities.

Youth need to collide with respected elders

"Don't be harsh or impatient with an older man. Talk to him as you would your own father. ...Reverently honour an older woman as you would your mother and the younger woman as your sister

1 Timothy 5:1-3(The Message)."

One of the great things about being in a community that worships all together is that our youth are always with our elders when we worship God. It certainly has given everyone a wider perspective of how different we are. Within that context we have all had to learn tolerance. We have an elderly man in our community who, well, let's just say is quite an individual. He has lived quite a difficult life and as a result can be a little rough around the edges. He has been known to say things that can sound offensive at times and yet there are pearls of wisdom that come from him if you are willing to listen. I know for a fact he has felt unwelcome in many church settings and it is nice to know he feels loved and accepted in our community. One thing I have been very impressed by is the way the youth are respectful and caring toward him. They have learned to get past the rough edges and see the real man. It has taught us all a lot about not judging but rather simply respecting elders.

---

56   Joiner, p.73.

There are other elderly women and men whom our youth have found incredibly inspiring. I remember one of our older wise women stood to share about what prayer meant to her. She went over the time I gave her, she spoke in great depth and I feared that it might have gone over the heads of most of the children. But, as she finished, a young girl aged ten applauded her as she sat down.

This was out of context as there was no other applause for others who had shared. It was just that the ten year old loved to hear this lady speak and was responding accordingly. I saw her get up after our time of sharing and walk straight over to the lady to thank her for sharing. It was a joy to see the generations learn, listen and appreciate each other. We need to be creating more and more environments where this can happen.

> *"The days when youth ministry focused only on teenagers are over. Since youth mirror the faith of the adults who love them, parents and congregations need sustained and intentional models for Christian maturity."*

"The days when youth ministry focused only on teenagers are over. Since youth mirror the faith of the adults who love them, parents and congregations need sustained and intentional models for Christian maturity."[57]

Parents need to collide with each other

> *"For this reason, ever since I heard about your faith in the Lord Jesus and your love all the saints, I have not stopped giving thanks for you, remembering you in my prayers. I keep asking that the God of our Lord Jesus Christ, the glorious father, may give you the spirit of wisdom and revelation so that you may know him better*
>
> *(Ephesians 1:15-17; NIV)."*

One of the sad things about our siloed lives is that we feel very isolated at times. We are supposed to walk this path together. Somehow a value has been passed down that we are not to show our struggles but must somehow

---

57   *Creasy-Dean, Kendra Jan/Feb 2009, Expanding The Umbrella, Group Magazine, p.60*

act as if everything is fine in our household. The fact is that if we get close enough to anyone we see that is not true. True collision requires that we are real with the whole of life. I have found it very comforting to do life with other families, especially when they have children a little older than mine. I get to see that so much of our family's struggles are normal or universal. I find talking to other mums helpful, encouraging and hopefully they feel the same way when I share with them. We are meant to encourage each other, share one another's burdens, and support each other. This was never meant to be a journey all alone, and sometimes that means there will be collisions both positive and negative.

"Everyone needs to be believed in by someone, and everyone needs to belong somewhere. True community provides both."[58]

Parents need to collide with Grandparents

"I will pour out my spirit on every kind of people. Your sons will prophecy, also your daughters. Your young men will see visions; your old men will dream dreams…Whoever calls out for help to me, God, will be saved
(Acts 2:17-18, 21; NIV)."

Perspective is one of the key things I always learn when I collide with the older generation. Sometimes I want to hear it, sometimes I don't, but it is always helpful. There is something very sad about a culture that shuts out the voices of multiple generations. I love these verses in Acts 2, as they speak of all voices being valued and used by God, speaking from different perspectives.

Over the past seven years in particular, as we have lived and served together, I have been more aware of these different perspectives. When our sons and daughters prophesy, they often see things that don't seem possible and have faith that can move mountains. Young men see visions, because they are still young enough to believe that things can change and they see big possibilities. When old men dream dreams, it is almost as though they have seen it all and have learnt there are some things that will only happen in our dreams, or on the other side of eternity. Each person has a voice and we

---

58   Joiner, p.186.

need to listen to each other. I am still a parent who believes I can make a difference. I appreciate my mother's wisdom. I listen when, every now and then, she says, "Learn to let go and love them no matter what they choose!" I need that collision in my parenting, even when I don't like what I hear. I am moving into a time of parenting where that will be vital. I will need her wisdom to help me parent well in this stage as my children enter the teenage years.

Singles need to collide with families.

"Each of you should look not to your own interests, but also to the interests of others

(Phil. 2:4; NIV)."

Paul said to the church in Philippi that they needed to look outside themselves. In the book of Titus, Paul presents a lengthy discourse about being married and single and concludes that this is simply a choice. Either way, we need to encourage and support each other regardless of our marital and family status. The fact is that we are all a part of the family of God and there is equal value and a place for us all.

One of the most common ministry separations I see in church communities is "singles ministry". While there is always value to meet with like-minded people, I will never forget Donald Miller speaking at a conference saying how special it was for him, a single man, to be able to go to a family's home for dinner once a week and feel a part of that family. He saw how a father interacted with his family. For Donald Miller, who was someone who didn't have such a positive role model in this area, this family experience was one he greatly valued. This wouldn't have happened if he was only going along to the singles' ministry at his church.

Over the years in ministry I have felt that people who are single, or single parent families, have felt not included when the term "family ministry" is being used. We must realise that this is an example where language can be a barrier. We need to break it down and open it up. We need to try really hard to support our singles and single parent families within our community, by making all that we do inclusive.

We have an amazing middle-aged single lady, who has not been able to have a family of her own due to difficult circumstances. Our children have demanded that she be their godparent. She loves children and longs to be around them. She is like a mother to so many of the children in our community. It is a gift she has. We are very careful not to use words like "family picnic" or "family camp" because she will immediately feel she is not welcome.

We aim to be sensitive with the way we speak and interact with each other so she doesn't feel left out. We are very intentional about making sure that she is always included in what would be considered traditional family time, such as Christmas, Birthdays, Mothers' day and Fathers' day. These can often be hard times for single, widowed or divorced people. A true "collision" needs to be aware of all the dynamics and we need to aim to be as inclusive as possible.

She is so special to us, and hopefully she feels the same way about us. She brings a different perspective to our lives because of the situation in which she finds herself. We enrich each other's lives when we "collide".

Families need to collide with families.

"Let us not give up meeting together, as some are in the habit or doing, but let us encourage one another —and all the more as you see the day approaching

(Heb. 10:25; NIV)."

Meeting together and encouraging each other can take so many forms. Whatever it looks like, it is meant to be real. I like the fact that when our life group stops meeting for the two weeks over the school holiday break, I get a text from one of the members saying, "Can't wait to catch up, have missed life group". That's the way it should be. When we meet it needs to be encouraging and life-giving. That means that we give and take with each other, and we need to make the effort to make sure that our collisions allow for that. Many traditional meetings consist of a few up front teaching, a lot of people taking and then many leaving with little or no interaction. In Acts 2, believers shared food and their belongings and no one wanted for anything. That is families colliding with families.

We have two families in particular that continue to give us strength and life as we "do life" together. I thank God for them regularly. They are families with similar passions to serve God with all their heart and mind and soul. Even though for each of us that expression looks different, that doesn't matter; it continues to challenge and polish each of us in our own walk of life. We also know without a doubt we will always be there for each other no matter what happens.

We choose to make strategic time together in the busy-ness of life. This is because we give each other strength to continue living the journey for God holistically, within our family. Every time we are together we walk away enriched and strengthened. Our children all love each other deeply and they also love the relationships they have with the adults. There are many times when we get together where our children go one way, and the adults go the other. But there are just as many times where all together we laugh and enjoy life, food and experiences. I believe these relationships have become our true anchors in all of our lives. This will be especially true for our children, for many years to come. I pray that every family has another family that they can do life with. It is vital for growing and feeling grounded to handle whatever life throws our way.

What collisions are you having that meet needs like that?

Villages need to collide with villages.

"'Look after him,' he said, 'and when I return ,I will reimburse you for any extra expense you may have.' Which of these three do you think was a neighbour to the man who fell into the hands of the robbers? The expert in the law replied, 'The one who had mercy on him.' Jesus told him, 'Go and do likewise.'

(Luke 10: 35b -37; NIV)."

The Good Samaritan in Luke 10 is a great reminder to us that we should be looking outside our own village, our own comfort zone, and helping others who are different from us. The power of this story is that the one who was hated helped his enemy, while the religious person just walked

> *A family in the Old Testament would have included parents, children, workers, andperhaps even adult siblings with their own spouses and children*

on by. Jesus was challenging the Pharisees about what was important to God. Villages helping other villages, even when they hate each other? Now that's a collision!

"A family in the Old Testament would have included parents, children, workers, and perhaps even adult siblings with their own spouses and children. In fact, households could be compiled of as many as eighty people. These texts, such as Deuteronomy 6, are discussing the communal raising of children. Our own cultural distance from these passages may cause us to put undue pressure on parents alone."[59]

Our village community has made a deliberate collision with a village in Cambodia. As relationships have developed over the last four years, many of our community feel very connected to this small village and the people that are there. One year we took pieces of paper with pictures and stories from people in our community, sharing a bit of ourselves to the villagers over there. They were so touched by this that they did the same. So we brought back thirty pieces of paper from Cambodians sharing their likes, dislikes and passions. Many of them said things like, "We love you so much and feel like we have a family in Australia. Thank you for all you do for us, we pray for you every day". Believe me, when they say they pray for you, they really do!

The fact that we have Cambodians praying for us here in Australia is an incredible blessing, for their faith is a constant inspiration and challenge to us. As for them, it is all they have sometimes. We need their prayers, as so much here distracts us from the important things. So, each year we feel a greater connection and our response is to help as much as we can, for we are resource rich and can contribute much in that area. We definitely feel we receive as much, if not more, than we give, from being connected and committed to this village in Cambodia.

---

59   Miller, Meredith 5 Sept, 2007, *Family Ministry: Good things come in threes, Fuller Youth Institute,* http://fulleryouthinstitute.org/2007/09/family-ministry/

We all need to collide with GOD

*"I'm speaking to you out of deep gratitude for all, that God has
given me, and especially as I have responsibilities in relation
to you. Living then, as every one of you does, in pure grace, it's
important that you not misinterpret yourselves as people who
are bringing this goodness to God. No, God brings it all to you.
The only accurate way to understand ourselves is by what God
is and by what He does for us, not by what we are and what
we do for Him.*

Romans 12:3-6 (The message)

In this way we are like the various parts of a human body. Each part gets
its meaning from the body as a whole, not the other way around. The body
we're talking about is Christ's body of chosen people. Each of us finds our
meaning and function as a part of his body

***Can it be any clearer that our purpose, strength and value come
only from God? It is Him with whom we all need to collide.***

Time to Collide:

You cannot lead where
you have not gone yourself.

Take some time out to consider the following questions in your own context.

1. What are the ways in which you allow, or see value, in "collisions" across the generations, within your family, your Christian community and the wider community in general?

_____

_____

_____

_____

_____

2. In your own life journey, can you think of a time when you have grown, or found value, in colliding with another person in another generation?

_____

_____

_____

_____

3. Consider the stories you are passing on. How can you be more strategic in doing that with the next generation in particular?

_____

_____

_____

_____

_____

4. Who is speaking into your life?   And whose lives are you speaking into?

_____

_____

_____

_____

_____

Chapter 4

Colliding on the 'faith' journey

"And Jesus grew in wisdom and stature, and in favour with God and men
(Luke 2:52; NIV)."

This verse talks about the time when Jesus was a child. At this time, we find Him in the temple, listening and asking questions of the teachers. It clearly states that he was twelve years old at the time.

Luke 2:52 seems to me to be an overriding statement that summarises His childhood. Jesus was growing into a mature man and he was very balanced. Luke 2:52 also stresses four key elements of a person's growth that are not mutually exclusive, but need to be in balance as we all grow and develop.

There are clearly four elements of the faith journey that are stated as keys to Jesus' maturing as a person. This process starts very early. In fact I would say, along with many other processes, it starts the moment you are born. His formative years were very important in relation to the rest of his life, and this is the same for everyone.

"Children are not things to be moulded, but people to be unfolded." [60]

Jesus did not just spend his first twelve to eighteen years until he could become God. He always was God, and the early years were just as important as any other years of His life. The sooner we start to treat children as people "being unfolded", the sooner we will begin to understand the lifelong journey of a person as a spiritual being. We will see discipleship as more long term and holistic.

If you consider the many stories of people's lives in the Bible, and the events where

> *"Children are not things to be moulded, but people to be unfolded."*

Boyd. C, 1994

people were growing and serving God, you will find that children were in the midst of much of what was happening. I challenge you to re-read the stories of the Flood, the tower of Babel, the Exodus, the feeding of the 5000, and the triumphal entry of Christ, through the eyes of a child who was there. You will find that they were present right alongside the adults. They were there when the manna fed them every day, when the languages came and when they were fed by two fish and five loaves. The children were impacted by these experiences as much as the adults. So much of their faith journey was being unfolded by the experience of growing up with life happening around them.

If you were to look at all aspects of the faith journey – acts of service, worship of God, acts of spiritual fellowship, and confessions of faith through the normal and the supernatural – children were there. I challenge you to think about the places where you would have found children throughout the stories of the Bible. They are people to be unfolded, not simply moulded.

Let us break down these four key elements of Luke 2:52:

"And Jesus grew in **wisdom** and **stature**, and in **favour with God and men**" Luke 2:52

Wisdom: Actively GROWING in God's wisdom.

Stature: Belonging and living in a COMMUNITY.

Favour with God: HONOURING God and recognising the place of awe that He deserves as our Creator.

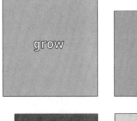

Favour with Men: Having the opportunity to SERVE the world around us as we understand our faith and call in this world.

Wisdom: Actively Growing in God's wisdom.

We see here that Jesus naturally grew intellectually. This is an important process. There is much growth in this area during the first twelve years of a person's life. We learn to speak, read, write, reason and understand how life works. Of course we must never stop learning, but there is much research to show that it is the first seven to eight years that are vital to the foundation that forms a person's belief system. A child asks a hundred and forty four questions a day when they are young. Once they become adults, that drops to approximately twenty questions a day. [61]

It is vitally important to grow up with God's worldview as your foundation. Of course there are many people today who have never grown up with this. But, there is a clear difference between learning intellectually in isolation and learning in collision with the other three elements. This is where education, and especially the traditional program known as "Sunday School", has often missed a vital key to how we develop.

For example, if I wanted to teach someone how to ride a bicycle there are several techniques I could opt for. I could sit them down in a classroom setting and show them a picture of a bicycle. I could break the bicycle down and teach them every aspect of how a bicycle works. I could share my experiences of what I do when I ride a bicycle. I could even test them on all I have taught and they could get a hundred percent in the test about riding a bicycle. Does that mean they know how to ride one?

When we deal with intellectual development in isolation this is the result we get: people who have lots of information about topics but still have not developed to a healthy maturity in any subject.

Of course there is always a place for formal education, and intellectual stimulation. The fact that Jesus was in the temple interacting and asking questions is a classic example of Jesus knowing His scriptures, and being able to converse intelligently about issues with the Priests. He needed more than just straight factual and intellectual lessons. Here we find him debating and trying to understand through conversation and interaction.

Stature: Belonging and living in a COMMUNITY

Jesus grew physically. He learned skills, which meant that he played a role in the family and the village in which he lived. It is documented that he

---

61   Hanna, Tim 2011, "Leaders To Go" conference, Qld, Australia..

71

was a carpenter; he was good with his hands and building things. I think that when it comes to community in the western world, and especially in big cities, we have lost a little of the understanding of what it would have been like to belong to a community. I know this is still very strong in small country towns and it can happen in the city; we just have to try harder to create opportunities. However, we don't tend to be as holistic as I believe God first intended. I think of the old sitcom *Cheers*, where a community was formed around a little bar." Its theme song was, *Where Everybody Knows Your Name* by Gary Portnoy and Judy Hart AngeloIn a 2011 Readers Poll in Rolling Stone magazine, "Where Everybody Knows Your Name" was voted the best television theme of all time[62] . Who can forget the lyrics?

Where everybody knows your name, and they're always glad you came.

You wanna be where you can see, our troubles are all the same

You wanna be where everybody knows your name

> *We are created to be connected, understood and known by a small group of people*

When I was in the Cambodian village I caught a glimpse of what it might be like to be so close to others that everyone is affected by what is happening. All the children wandered around all day, being together, exploring together. Women would sit in the kitchen area all day, talking, cooking and laughing together. Men and women were out in the fields together working hard all day and many times the children would work alongside them. When they ate, it was likely that someone would drop in and join in. They would pool all the food and just spend time together.

We were only there for four days and four people had died in that time. No matter where you were in the village, you knew who had died and where the funeral was. Most daily life stopped for the funeral and most people were there celebrating that person's life. No matter where you were in the village you could hear the celebrations. Everyone played a role in the village and brought their gifts and skills for the benefit of all. When someone was

---

62   Portnoy, G & Hart, J, 2004, *Where everybody knows your name*, Album "keeper", http://www.garyportnoy.com/, USA

hungry, they received help; when someone was sick, they received help. The pastor we stayed with seemed to be the "go to" person for whatever the villagers needed. How wonderful for Christ's representative to be the "go to" person for the village.

It reminded me of how easily it would have been for Jesus' parents to lose their child as they were walking home from the temple. They would have naturally thought that he was with someone else because for them, like the Cambodians, "it takes a village to raise a child". These are elements of what I believe true community is meant to look like.

There was something about that community that made us Westerners feel we had so much to learn. We are created to be connected, understood and known by a small group of people. Imagine being in a place where people know you while you are growing up.

Recently I went to wedding. There were about two hundred people and it was out on a beautiful property in the country. There were people there from my first church community. There were people that spanned the whole forty three years of my life, including my spiritual and social life in my formative years. For many reasons life had meant that we had all gone our different ways. For many of us we were seeing people we hadn't seen in twenty to thirty years.

The bride was two and a half hours late, but do you think anyone cared? (Maybe the groom did). Everyone else was so happy to be together again, no one wanted to leave. Even in the two and a half hours I couldn't get around to everyone I wanted to speak with. I remember seeing one lady who, when I was around seven years old, took me under her wing, loved me, and encouraged me to sing and serve God. When we saw each other we hugged and cried. It was just as special for her to see me as it was for me to see her. There was so much sharing, community and love because we had seen each other grow and had been there in those formative years together. I heard the comment over and over again, "This is church. This is what it is all about. No one wants to leave; it is so wonderful to be together again."

Community is precious and important; it helps us grow physically as well as in every other aspect of life. We cannot do it in isolation. Yet, for so many

Australians their community is their local pub, RSL or café. The pubs and clubs meet the social need and the desire to not feel isolated. For others it is the workplace or the place where they have a hobby or passion.

For some, church can become a community where they feel they belong and that is a wonderful thing. It should be a place where everybody knows your name; a place where you can grow up and feel there are people encouraging you along the way. My church community was certainly that for me in my formative years. We simply need to be careful that it is not at the exclusion, or in isolation, of the other areas of development. Unfortunately many of our youth groups in Australia are full of young people that are there for their social fill and it never goes any further than that.

Favour with God: Honouring God and recognising the place of awe that He deserves as our Creator.

In Luke, chapter 2, Jesus' response to his parents when they found him in the temple was, "Why are you looking for me? Didn't you know that I had to be here, dealing with the things of my Father?" (The Message)

Jesus was brought up in a culture and family that had God at the centre of their life and world. They made a special effort to honour God on special occasions, such as the Feast of the Passover. They would have travelled as a family, most likely with many from their village. As a result he grew in favour with God. This was an important preparation for the rest of His life.

Honouring God is the area that seems to be most clearly defined in the western world. It is commonly known as a church service. This is a place where you can go to honour and worship God. In many countries there is a sense of awe that comes from being in old, ornate churches and monuments that have been erected to give honour to God. You don't have to look far to see these in all shapes and sizes.

The Old Testament is filled with altars and places that were named as sacred. Jesus would have been surrounded with those places regularly, as well as at the special feast times of the year that the whole village celebrated.

Living in Australia, which I believe is largely a non-Christian country; you have to look hard for such places. I realised how true that was when I was recently in Lebanon and every four hours the bells rang and chanting began. No matter where you were in the city you could hear the bells calling people to pray. I must admit I was very overcome with emotion to see how passionate and prevalent the Muslim faith is to their people, and how we have lost that sense as Christians that God is to be honoured in every part of our lives. It was of such importance that they would stop five times a day, wherever they were, to remember Allah.

In the Muslim faith, this is not something you simply do for an hour on one day of the week. This is something that effects your everyday life: when you walk, when you sleep, when you eat, when you dress, you honour him. Of course Deuteronomy 6:4 says this is the way we are meant to live the faith journey. It seems we have so often isolated this area of our faith to a Sunday morning service. We have compartmentalized it in our busy lives.

When Luke 2:52 talks about Jesus growing in favour with God, it meant Jesus walked with God daily. In fact when Jesus finally started His ministry at the age of thirty, the first thing He did was to go out in the desert and spend forty days with His father, for He knew from where His guidance and strength needed to come. He was constantly balancing the work of ministry with time with God.

When the disciples came to Him one day asking why He wasn't out talking to the people, they found Him spending time with God. They thought He needed to be spending more time with the people, healing and teaching them. Jesus knew that time with His father was important and, in fact, He felt guided by God to leave that town and go to another. He obeyed His father and they left. (Mark 1:35-39) Another time He said, "I tell you the truth, the Son can do nothing by himself; he can do only what he sees his Father doing, because whatever the Father does the Son also does (John 5:19)." There is an awe and reverence there that certainly shows that He knew His place. Imagine if we only spoke the words that we felt came from God?

Favour with Men: Have the opportunity to serve the world around us as we understand our faith and call in this world.

Jesus grew up (as it says in Luke) "obediently" with His parents and in the village. If you are in favour with men, then there must be respect and value in the relationships. We are challenged to live amongst family and neighbours and love them as we would love ourselves. As a child, Jesus needed to learn the social skills to live closely amongst other people. He could not have had the impact with people around Him, when He started His ministry, if He didn't have some integrity and strength of character as He was growing up.

When He began His ministry it was largely centred on helping people and serving them. Some of His final words to His disciples were all about serving others and putting others first. He lived this example all of His life and then at the Passover, when He washed their feet, He encouraged the disciples to live the way He did.

"I have taken my place among you as the one who serves
(Luke 22:28)."

We are called to serve and give to others. We are called to put others first before our own needs and to love them the way God loves them. It is a high calling. We, like Jesus, should be known for our love and the way we serve others. It is an important part of our Christian walk and it starts as soon as we are able. It needs to be an outworking of who we are in Christ, not an isolated act.

Very rarely was there a time when Jesus served, that did not affect people socially, intellectually, physically and spiritually. Sometimes we can serve someone in the community and it can be an isolated act. While it is still valuable it can be so much more powerful when it comes within community relationships and with Christ at the centre.

There are many good causes out there: saving animals, serving the hungry, restoring houses from floods and fire. They are all the correct human responses to difficult times. It is sad that, in isolation, they are often seen as a random act of kindness that many are often suspicious about, rather than an opportunity to shine hope and faith into something beyond the needs of today.

Again it was refreshing to see in Cambodia that effective serving of others in the village came from the Christians. They did not want to just help the people with hunger, health and education. A natural outcome was that people were hungry to understand and hear about Jesus. There was a collision of needs all being met at the same time.

There is no doubt we are called to serve each other and with that must come an ability to earn respect and integrity among our fellow man. This is a sign of a mature person.

All of these elements are important in their own right but, most importantly, they are meant to be developed in collision with each together. If we are going to see transformation in a person's faith journey there has to be more of a collision of these elements right throughout life.

> *The dropout problem is , at its core, a faith development problem. To use religious language, it's a disciple-making problem*

I believe it is the isolation that has stunted the growth of the Christian faith in the Western World in particular. It has certainly stunted our children's growth and they are the next generation of people who are going to lead the world. We are simply losing them. As David Kinnaman in his book, *You lost me – why young Christians are leaving church and re-thinking faith* he says, "The dropout problem is , at its core, a faith development problem. To use religious language, it's a disciple-making problem. The church is not adequately preparing the next generation to follow Christ faithfully in a rapidly changing culture."[63]

The faith journey is transformational when we understand that God wants to be a part of every aspect of our life, and that we are designed to grow within community, with Christ at the centre. We are transformed when we love others as much as we love ourselves and when our foundation is one where we realise we can't do that without God's help.

---

63   Kinnaman, D. 2011, *You lost me – Why young Christians are leaving church and re-thinking faith*, Baker Books, Michigan, USA, p.21,

Time to Collide:

Take some time out to consider the following questions in your own context.

1. Consider the four key areas that Jesus grew in. How are you, personally, growing in the them?

   • Actively Growing in God's wisdom

   _____

   _____

   _____

   • Belonging and Living in a Community

   _____

   _____

   _____

   • Honouring God

   _____

   _____

   _____

- Having the opportunity to serve the world around-you

_____

_____

_____

2. Consider the four key areas that Jesus grew in. How are you as a leader creating environments in which people in your community can grow?

_____

_____

_____

3. Where the gaps and what are are the areas where you are doing well? Take some time to celebrate the wins and plan to bridge the gaps.

_____

_____

_____

_____

Chapter 5

What happens when we isolate the elements in the community of faith?

When we look at the current situation with the church and children today we have to ask why they are not coming to church anymore. Of course this can be said for adults in Australia as well, but for this book I am addressing the need to rethink the current situation in regards to our children.

While this is by no means exhaustive, I believe if we start to understand this issue it may help us be more effective in keeping our children on the journey of Christ and hopefully actually attracting many others.

In chapter 4, I outlined the key elements of maturing in Christ. I want to unpack with you what happens when we emphasize only one of them at the exclusion of the others. We have been guilty of focusing on a key area and in turn have ISOLATED or SILOED the other elements in church life into individual compartments rather than seeing that there is much more to be gained when we intentionally work on all keys areas at the same time.

LANGUAGE COUNTS

Before we unpack these key areas, I want to note the language. Until now I have been very careful to not use language that is currently used in churches all the time. I believe that if we are to be open to change and new collisions we need to understand that it is often our language that limits our thinking. Language is definitely a key stumbling block for those outside the church.

"Focusing on the way we say things, without regard to how we say it doesn't work in marriage, with our kids, in politics, or in any other social arrangement. So why do we think that it would work with God? Do we think he is happy with us for alienating his world?"[64]

 Halter, H. and Smay, M. YEAR, *The Tangible Kingdom* PUBLISHER, p.41

> *But the local church many have come to cherish – the services, offices, programs, buildings, and ceremonies – is neither Biblical nor unbiblical. It is a Biblical – that is – such an organization is not addressed in the Bible.*

For this chapter I will have to use language such as Sunday school, Worship Services, Discipleship and Fellowship because otherwise it will be so much harder to explain my meaning. But, please understand that one of the first things you are going to have to consider changing when you want to help people re-think the faith journey in your language.

The respected leader and writer George Barna also addresses this:

"You should realize that the Bible neither describes nor promotes the local church as we know it today. Many centuries ago religious leaders created a prevalent form of church that is so widespread in our society to help people be better followers of Christ. But the local church many have come to cherish – the services, offices, programs, buildings, and ceremonies – is neither Biblical nor unbiblical. It is a Biblical – that is – such an organization is not addressed in the Bible." [65]

What happens when we isolate the elements in the community of faith?

ISOLATION IS THE ISSUE

When something is done in isolation, there are elements of our journey of faith that might be unhealthy. They take the focus, things get out of balance and then we find that other areas are not being developed. Even important elements can become out of balance and this hinders our development. Something is missing.

Let's look at the four elements on the faith journey as outlined in Chapter 4 and see what they can look like when they are isolated.

1. When community is in isolation, we are in danger of becoming a Kids' Club.

For other age groups this will be called a social club of some sort. For your community it may be a Craft group, Youth group, Men's shed, Playgroup

---

65   Barna, G. 2005, Revolution, Tyndale Publishing, pg 37.

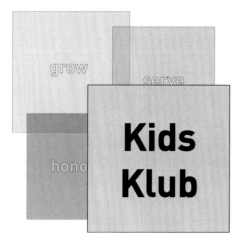

etc. There are many such programs and ministries within the church today. This is where the social need of a certain demographic of people can be fulfilled. They can get together and have some fun.

A club is a very easy way to reach out to children and it is an easy access point for children to come along. You can find that you are running a program where you are attracting hundreds of children and they are all having a wonderful time at your Kids' Club.

This major program can be largely social. You may feed them, you probably play games and do craft and special activities occasionally. The children who come along to the club will generally be around the same age and mostly they will interact with their peers in this context. You may have some spiritual input which may run from five minutes up to thirty minutes.

As a children's pastor, I ran a Kids' Club which was the largest program happening at the church at the time. We had hundreds of children from the ages of eight to twelve years. We had significant teaching (thirty minutes) and aimed to have older leaders running games, food and craft.

It was successful. It was a safe, loving place that we were providing for the children who came. However, I would have to say that only a handful of those children are still walking on the faith journey with God. Most came in, had fun and left when they found something better.

It was largely an isolated program with very little challenge for service, worship and real personal growth with God for the children. It was an isolated ministry in a larger church structure. Most people had no idea it even existed and there was very little cross-over into other aspects of church life.

Am I saying it was a waste of time? NO!

Am I saying if I understood the need to collide the elements we might have been more effective in helping the children stay on the faith journey? YES!

2. When growth is in isolation, it can become just about head knowledge and we are in danger of looking like a 20th Century Sunday School.

When you say the word Sunday school, there is a universal understanding of what it looks like today. It is usually a small group, but it can be a larger classroom setting, where Bible truth is taught. Some groups may have some music, some may have some craft, some may have small group discussion and some may have a take home sheet. All will have a story or some sort of teaching of truth from the Bible.

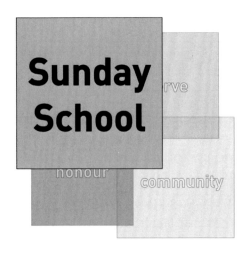

Sunday school is almost always done with the same age groups, with an older, wiser teacher leading the group. They are mostly held on Sundays and for children in Australia they are mostly held at the same time as a Sunday service which their parents attend. They are sometimes teaching the same truth as adult church, but this is not always the case. The major teaching method is intellectual and taught in a school type fashion, hence the name 'Sunday School'. There are prizes for attendance and for remembering memory verses and, sometimes, even for bringing a friend.

The Sunday Schools I have just described are usually in isolation from the challenge of service, and don't have much structured time to be social. Sunday school emphasizes intellectual growth and learning but often there is little challenge for application. Remember my explanation about teaching a person to ride a bike? Unless we put it into action, we have to ask: what have we truly learned?

Because children have been taught in isolation, there is often no continued communication between parents and children about what they have learned and very little shared application from Sunday to Sunday.

The statistics will show that many children growing up in Sunday school programs are concluding, by the age of ten, that Jesus is boring and irrelevant and they are getting out of Sunday school as soon they are allowed.

> *The statistics will show that many children growing up in Sunday school programs are concluding, by the age of ten, that Jesus is boring and irrelevant and they are getting out of Sunday school as soon they are allowed*

"We have to seriously consider that leaving Christian education to a Sunday School setting only removes faith from context and weakens the likelihood of lifelong discipleship, as such separation of children form adults gives an artificial understanding of the Christian walk."[66]

Am I saying it is a waste of time? NO!

Am I saying that if we understood the need to collide the elements, we might be more effective in helping the children stay on the faith journey? YES!

3. When service is in isolation, it becomes duty-driven and/or can be seen as humanist or a form of social justice.

This is often seen in Para-church organizations where the need to feed and clothe the homeless becomes the driver for everything they do. Some churches and denominations have become known for the role they play in the community because it is such a big part of what they do. It becomes a place where people feel pressured to continue to serve, sometimes at the expense of their own faith journey or their families.

Even Jesus, at times, had to walk away from service because of the need to be with His father. Service in isolation can deplete us emotionally, physically and spiritually. Many people leave the church because they are burnt-out and feel overused. It is difficult to achieve balance because as Jesus said,

---

66   *Alexander, L. 2012, Children, families and God, Evangelista Media, Italy, p.64.*

Social Justice

"The poor will always be with us (reference)". The needs are so great and they are very overwhelming, but service in isolation is a sure-fire killer of anyone's faith journey.

When it comes to children, the interesting thing is that we seem to have isolated them from serving. We don't believe they can do it and this has been detrimental to our children's faith journey.

My own children have taught me about service, just as much as anyone else. I remember preparing my children to do mission work in the Cambodian village and setting the boundaries about what they could and couldn't do. We were in the slums one day helping a team there feed, clean and teach the children in the middle of the street. I was asked to wash the children, so there I was in the middle of the street, washing these little children's bodies and their nit infested hair. I felt very embarrassed for them as their parents were too busy gambling in the tents around me to care what I was doing with their children. I tried to be ever so respectful as I washed their hair. I felt so sad that this was what their life had come to. All of a sudden I could hear my daughter's voice and little hands pushing me from behind saying, "Hey, Mum, let me help. Move over".

I wanted to isolate her from this experience; to protect her. But, she was determined and pushed her way in along with another of the young people we had brought with us. I went to dry my hands and grab the camera to take a picture. There they were making funny designs with the children's hair. They were all laughing and having a lovely time.

When we isolate our children from serving, we don't allow them and others (namely me!) to grow. My daughter taught me a lot about serving that day. But if service is done in isolation we are in danger of feeling as though that good work stops our guilt. We can then do what we like. Going to Cambodia changed the way our family thinks and responds to the opulence of our environment. I believe this can only come from Christ's prompting, and with our service being done within a holistic paradigm. The good deed does not stop there; it transforms and changes us into different people.

If service is in isolation from the other elements, or if it is isolating certain people from serving, then we need to realize we could be stunting what God wants to teach us in a more holistic fashion.

Am I saying it is a waste of time to serve in isolation? NO!

Am I saying that if I understood the need to collide the elements, it might be more effective in helping our children stay on the faith journey? YES!

4. When honouring is in isolation, we are in danger of becoming "one day a week Christians", and out of touch with the real world.

We are in danger of becoming Sunday Christians, with the Sunday service the main way to express our faith. The fear is that we can become removed from the world we live in. For example, a man said to me, "We spend all of our time teaching kids to pray in tongues and being slain in the spirit. I never thought to go out and mow someone's lawn".

In Australia, it is interesting to ask where the average Australian is on a Sunday morning. I know where they are not. They are not in church. They are in bed with a hangover; they are mowing the lawn; they're at the beach; they're playing sport; they're at the park, or at Bunning's home hardware store. I am not trying to make a judgment on Australians, but rather trying to challenge us all as Christians. Are we not meant to be the light of the world? When my son, Sam, was twelve he read in the Bible about us being

the light of the world and how we need to not put a bucket over the light and hide it. His first response to me was, "Well if that is so, why are we inside the Church building every Sunday? Isn't that hiding our light where only the Christians can see it?"

There can also be isolation amongst believers in the Church, even when we are together. I spent time with a pastor recently who was hurting and burnt-out. He said, "I go to this particular church, because I can sneak in and sneak out and no one talks to me. It's the way I like it". When honouring God simply becomes a service we attend once a week, we are in danger of not growing and transforming into all that He would want for us.

The other important point, when we are talking about children, is that we mostly isolate them from the adult experience. We create their own honouring experience, with the desire to make it more age appropriate. It often means that the first time they enter adult church is when they are youth and/or adults and it is all new to them. It is often so foreign to them that it is often their excuse to stop coming. Another scenario is that they only go to adult church in the school holidays and they are mostly given a sheet to do quietly up the back of the building. The message to the children then is that you are not welcome in God's presence unless you are an adult and you can be quiet.

Of course we are called to worship Him and there are many ways to do that. A church worship service is certainly a key one. But, if it is always done in isolation from serving the community; experiencing real community amongst believers (some would call that fellowship), and deeply growing towards Christ (some would call that discipleship) then we are in danger of not seeing true transformation in our lives.

Am I saying a church service is a waste of time? NO!

Am I saying that if we understand the need to collide the elements, we might be more effective in helping everyone stay on the faith journey? YES!

In its simplest form I am talking about gaining a balance. Most people would agree that while no single program can fulfil everyone's needs, at the very least we need to make sure that our faith journey has a balance of the four elements. A healthily structured faith community will make sure that everyone has an opportunity to develop across the four elements in a balanced way.

At another level I am challenging us all to think what would it look like if we considered structuring (or more accurately it may mean re-structuring) and creating environments where there can be a collision of the four elements all at the same time. It is actually more possible than you think. I will go one step further and say that I believe not only did Jesus model it, but that it is central to seeing lives transformed in Christ and central to the mission of Christ.

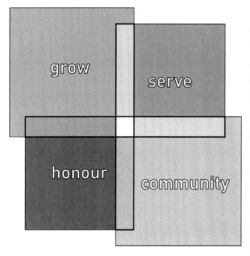

Jesus spent three years in ministry, mainly with twelve people: living, eating, serving, teaching and showing them how to live a life that could be transformed. Many of His teachings came out of a need or an experience which they stumbled upon as they walked and played together as a band of brothers. They did life together and, as they did, Jesus lived in such a way that His life transformed them all. So much so that when He left them they carried the ministry on. Did they always understand? No. Did they always know what they were doing? No. Did they always know what Jesus was doing? No. Did the disciples make mistakes? Yes. Did Jesus ever give up on them? No.

I encourage you to take some time out and revisit how Jesus discipled His disciples. The rest of this book will explore what this can look like. I challenge you to re-think what an environment would look like in your context where these four key elements collide together. I believe this can, at least, start to help our children's faith journey become deeply rooted in Christ. But there are some other key elements we must add. We will look at them later but, before we do, take some time to collide in a few issues raised in this chapter.

Time to Collide:

Take some time out to consider the following questions in your own context.

When Jesus walked this earth:

How long did He take before He sent the disciples out on their own?

_____

How much time did He spend teaching in the religious places? And, what did He teach there?

_____

_____

How did He spend His time?

_____

_____

When were the most teachable times for His disciples?

_____

_____

What environments was He in when transformation was happening in the disciples' lives?

_____

_____

What ministries are done in ISOLATION within your Church?

_____

_____

How are your children, in particular isolated from the rest of the Church?

_____

_____

You might like to begin a conversation with your key leaders about how they see the current structure, and consider what are its pros and cons.

_____

_____

List the benefits of your current structure and the barriers created by your current structure. Match this to your findings on the way Jesus discipled his followers and the way He did ministry while He was on this earth.

_____

_____

Chapter 6

Called to collide.

We have looked at the key elements in detail and what happens when they become isolated in a faith community. If we were to bring the four elements together and overlap them, we would see the place where we need to focus.

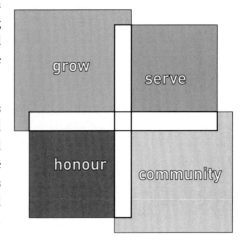

The focus is where the elements overlap. The sweet spot, the small square in the middle, is where all four elements overlap and where effectiveness of transformation is increased. When we overlap all four elements we see the cross. The mission becomes clear.

The Mission of Christ in John 3:16: "For God so loved the world that He gave His only son that whoever believes in Him shall not perish but have eternal life".

The commission in Matthew 28:19-20: "Therefore go and make disciples of all nations, baptizing them in the name of the Father, and the Son and the Holy Spirit and teaching them to obey everything I have commanded you. And surely I am with you always, to the very end of the age".

What does it mean to be missional?

Mission means "Enculturation"; to embody the Gospel. It means to take the worlds of others as seriously as they do and helping them find Christ there. We must do that in our families and then they will become contagious.

"Not to be swayed by the culture, but to sway the culture."

For me to say "Missional church" is like saying "people, people". I think it is saying the same word twice. Why do we not get it that it is the same word? It has the same meaning and the same purpose!

The mission of love must compel us (2 Corinthians 5:14-15) to go out into the world and live and talk about what Christ has done for us. We are called to fulfil the Great Commission: to make disciples, to go, to live and obey His commands.

1. When the mission compels community.

Mission compels the social club mentality to change and move toward a purpose and desire that is bigger than just meeting together for our own purposes.

"Creating intentional opportunities for young and old to meet together, to share stories, to create something together or merely to talk can be mutually beneficial and can bless the whole body of Christ.[67]"

Within our own community, there was a safe and comfortable feeling. We enjoyed being together as an extended family. As we were challenged by the mission of Christ, and as His love compelled us, we knew our "connect" events (our social connection time) had to become so much more.

We realised that our passion for family and being together was a gift we needed to share. We had already begun a ministry called "Southern Cross Club". This was a place where disadvantaged children were invited to be a part of a special club once a month. Our faith community has banded together to create a safe place where one-on-one mentoring can happen and where extended family is created for children whose families are dysfunctional. But, we wanted to take it a step further and to open up our "connect" events to the families of the SCC children.

> *Not to be swayed by the culture, but to sway the culture*

---

67   Allen, Holly C & Ross, Christine L, 2012, "Intergenerational Christian Transformation", Intervarsity Press, USA, pg 141.

This meant that the families of these children came into an environment where we could build relationships, model healthy family communication, show love, and serve them any way possible. Now we find ourselves eating and spending time amongst wife beaters, lesbians and drug addicts and have a chance to shine God's light as best we can. I am very aware that not all faith communities will be in a position of trust and privilege that enables them to meet and be caring towards such people, who would normally never walk into a church building. These families love that fact that we do so much for their children and their family, and they willingly come.

> *Creating intentional opportunities for young and old to meet together, to share stories, to create something together or merely to talk can be mutually beneficial and can bless the whole body of Christ*

This is how our social group, compelled by mission, has become a place where we can actively love and care for people who do not yet know Christ. While this is sometimes hard for our families, it is the mission that keeps us on track. It came out of asking, "How can we strategically create an environment where all ages can be together and we can serve and love and get to know each other better?"

It is what I call a collision driven by mission.

2. When the mission compels growth.

When we are compelled by a love for mission it actually heightens the desire to learn. As a pastor, I love the fact that if I am going to be of any help to others, I need to study and understand more and more. But I find the most value in learning because I am doing it for a greater purpose: the mission of Christ.

When we empower anyone on the faith journey to actually start putting his or her faith into action, the learning curve will increase dramatically. Most people say they don't share their faith because they don't know how. But it is often more about lack of opportunity to do so. This is especially the case when learning is restricted to classroom lectures or Sunday sermons. In isolation, learners are not required to put anything into action. There is a general belief that because I am the paid professional, it is my job to do the mission of the church. As pastors, we must be willing to answer for allowing this belief to develop and giving into to it. I am not in my role to be or do everything. I am in my role to empower everyone to do something. It is definitely the model that Jesus left us with.

I have a teenage son. I know how hard it is to get teens to want to learn anything. So, of course, I was surprised when he and his best mate begged us to get together every Sunday night to learn more about the Gospel message, a couple of months before we went to Cambodia. All of a sudden the mission compelled them to want to learn. Now he is in a small group with others aged between thirteen to twenty years and together they talk about the deepest faith issues and he loves it.

When they got together and talked about what they wanted this group to be about, a few of them said that they wanted to talk about how they could reach out and serve others. Here is a group of teens, socializing together, learning about God and compelled by mission. They said very strongly that what they didn't want it to be was a "standard Youth Group".

It is what I call a collision driven by mission.

3. When mission compels honouring.
When you seek a collision driven by mission, you need to look at the gifting and skills that God has placed in your community and believe that He will want to use them in a unique way. I know it will look different for everyone and that is what makes it so exciting.

In our faith community, we are surrounded by people gifted in the creative arts. Now, the creative arts is a scary place, because in the world it is all about being famous, being noticed and being the centre of attention. So, to create a creative arts company that is compelled by the mission is not original, but it is not easy.

But the mission must compel us or we will be no different to either a social club – such as your local theatre company – an in-house worship-fest. Our arts company "Xarts" was born. We have, at the moment, a company of twenty five people, their ages ranging from seven to fifty three years old, working across the generations to create presentations that give both enjoyment and bring a challenge to all ages. The productions all have a very strong Christian message.

> *We refine our character by working with each other, and have learned to work with all different kinds of people that we might not always agree with*

There is growth in everyone as we refine our gifts. We refine our character by working with each other, and have learned to work with all different kinds of people that we might not always agree with. We are learning more about truth as we write and work through the Biblical principles and stories we want to convey.

We have had to lean on God, because so many times things have fallen apart and we find ourselves on our knees crying out to God for help. As a result of what we are doing we get to worship God regularly in song and dramatic presentation, which has been, personally, very challenging. In the past three years we have been able to share the Gospel message to thousands of people in Australia and beyond. It has become for us our spiritual act of worship, while serving in the mission of Christ.

It is what I call a collision driven by mission.

4. When the mission compels serving.

When mission compels serving we see the value in doing something other-centred. It is about serving for a higher purpose, rather than for us to feel good about ourselves. It is about regarding the eternal more highly than the immediate gratification. It is about giving the honour to God, rather than doing it in our own strength. It is about being part of bringing a piece of heaven down here to earth and seeing lives changed forever.

In this world of the quick fix, we must become a people who are there for the long haul. It is so easy to run in, dump something and leave. This would make us feel good about ourselves, yet not really change anything for people in the long run.

When serving is a quick fix, I fear we do more damage than good. The mission must compel us to prayerfully consider how best to serve, not in isolation but rather in relationship; in community; in God's strength and with the right knowledge.

It is about making a good investment with your resources and time and about empowering people to become independent rather than dependant on you in order for them to move on.

It is often about doing less, but doing something well. It is not always responding to the immediate need, but rather being compelled by the greater call. This is hard for people with servant hearts, who see a need and simply want to fill it all the time.

We have one beautiful person who struggles with this all the time. When we work with the children of Southern Cross Kids, the needs are always great. Sometimes these families, both parents and children, have learned that if they just keep pleading poor they can get people to give them everything. There is no sense of responsibility to make better decisions which will get them out of their current situation. It is like the old saying, 'Give a man a fish and you feed him for a day; teach him to fish and you feed him for life'.

One lady in our community is so driven by wanting to serve, that she constantly breaks the rules and gives the children and parents things she shouldn't. We have to talk about it constantly and help her to see the bigger picture. Just recently she had an experience that made her re-think this issue. She had been dropping off food to a family for a few weeks. One particular time she landed there with food at 9 am in the morning, on a week day. The children were still in bed and not at school; the mother was drunk on the lounge, and the house looked like a pigsty. She realized that while she keeps feeding them without any effort on their part, she is not helping them at all.

Because we are driven by mission, incidents like these have caused us to re-think how best to serve these families. We are looking to create life skills and tutoring ministry in which we offer these families weekly help in order that they may have the skills to help themselves. We are very excited about this ministry and know that it is going to be a long haul. It will require a lot of commitment. It will take the whole community time to be physically, mentally, socially and spiritually able to achieve this. A collision driven by mission will be transforming for all involved.

When mission collides with serving, it helps us to make choices about the things we must do and the things we can do. When mission helps us collide with the other elements we see that a relational community, honouring God with our gifts and service, and guiding others to learn more about God, strengthens serving.

Let me tell you a story that has been seven years in the making. A little girl called Ange came to one of the Southern Cross Kids' Camp: a camp for abused children. She was eight years old. She was jittery, wild, full of energy and exhausting for her buddy. These camps create a week of wonderful memories and a safe place for abused children. I've always felt it was cruel to give them a taste of something wonderful and then send them home again. However, the mission compels us to serve in community, with Christ at the centre of each message and for eternal purposes.

Each year she would come back and we saw her grow and change and blossom into a beautiful girl. In her last year of camp, her leadership potential was evident to me. She loved to help the little girls younger than herself and was so caring and protective towards her siblings. On the last day of her last camp, she got up in front of all the children and said, "I am going to miss this camp so much. All I can say to anyone here for the first time is to stay as long as you can, because these buddies of yours truly love you."

The next year we started up SCC, to be able to have ongoing mentoring throughout the year. It was the mission that compelled us to serve with this part of the community for the long haul. We knew it was going to be hard, but we really felt that it was not enough to have a week at camp. It was even harder seeing the children graduate and move onto nothing, when mostly their home life was just as difficult as ever.

I met up with Ange again, when she was fifteen years of age. One of her younger siblings started to come to club and she asked if she could come along to serve in the role of a "cousin". She wanted to give back something as camp had given her so much. I agreed and she has been serving for the last seven months.

At each club gathering I do some teaching on a godly character trait that might help the children as they grow up under difficult circumstances. They also spend time sharing. Ange came up to me recently after a teaching time and asked if she could talk to me. She was very embarrassed and stumbled with her words. She said, "I know this sounds silly, but when you talk I want to know more. I feel like I can talk to you and love to listen to you sharing. I know you are a busy person but...no, it is silly. I am sorry..."

I stopped her and said, "What you are saying is that you want to know more about Jesus and you would like to know if I would mentor you and be there as someone you can talk to about anything". She said "Yes" with tears in her eyes. I told her it would be my honour and privilege. We have been meeting in the afternoons and she is so hungry to learn and know more about God. I started the first mentoring session by giving her the book of Mark and challenged her to read the first chapter. I said the next time we got together we could talk about what she had read. When we met again, she gave me the book back and said, "I've finished that book. What's the next one?"

Since our meeting together she has been baptized and this year she is came to SCKC to serve as a cousin. This means she is completing the cycle, back where she started at camp, but now as a leader in the mission. You have no idea how excited she was to serve and help others come to know more about God. At the training meetings before camp I asked her to share with all the leaders about what it is like to be a camper at camp.

She shared that, for her, camp was the first place she learned that she could trust an adult. Because of this she decided she could try trusting others adults and eventually she came to put her trust in Christ. She shared that she was coming to camp to give to other children because of what she had been given. She challenged and moved everyone at the meeting that night.

But God is so good the story doesn't end there. At camp, she was walking along the track and a little girl ran up to her and wanted to hold her hand. As they walked along the track holding hands, she saw the little girl was a little sad. She said, "What's up?" The little girl said, "I'm feeling a little sad today and I wanted to talk to you, because you're someone I can trust." She was so overwhelmed. She felt that God was letting her know he can use her, too, in His mission.

Ange is a result of the "sweet spot" being hit. The four elements collided together and brought about transformation in a person's life. This was done through the power of the cross, and the message of the Gospel, being lived out by a small faith community.

It is what I call a collision driven by mission.

Creating a Culture of mission

Our children are very influenced by the culture in which they find themselves. It always amazes me how fads come and go; how they start, and how they become the thing that consumes children for a time. While it is dangerous to create a fad of mission that may come and go, I am amazed at how powerful and influential a culture can be. The question for me is: What is so powerful about it? And: How can we maintain this for our children to grow up in and be transformed?

How do we land that sweet spot right in the middle? How can we combine all those key elements together? How do we create a place where missional kids can be deeply rooted in Christ and live in that space? How do we make sure it is not just an event or a program that empowers them, but instead creates a culture of mission in their daily lives?

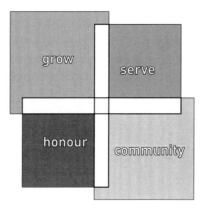

I remember the old Dunlop volley shoes that I wore when I was a kid. For a long time they were considered the cheap shoe that you had when you couldn't afford Nikes. Now they have become the fad. My own children want them as they are "cool" to wear. It is amazing how a shoe which seems to be not only cheap, but also structurally non-supportive for a child's developing feet, is now *the* shoe to wear.

I know that the Bible says, "There is nothing new under the sun (reference)", and fashion is mostly about selling clothes by recycling over a ten year cycle. But marketers use the power of peer culture, the influence youth have over each other, to dictate what is cool for the convenience of making money.

I have watched the influence of both bad and good role models in society create a whole fashion. For example, there was a young person who trashed his parent's house in Queensland in 2008. It made international news. During all the footage he wore dark sunglasses, with liquid paper on them. Pretty soon this became a huge fad. Behind it all is the powerful desire of young people to desperately fit in, belong and be a part of something bigger than themselves.

In our Xarts program ((X=Christian - Arts Program) we started working with children aged eight to twelve years. We found that once children turned twelve they didn't want to leave. We kept extending the age range, so as to include them. Maybe it is because creative arts crosses all age barriers, but now we find ourselves working with seven to eighteen year olds all together. In fact much of the time it is more like seven to fifty year olds working together. As a teacher, I know it breaks all the rules of teaching. I am surprised that the teenagers would even want to be a part of this culture we have created. When I ask them why they want to come, they say, "You give us opportunities to serve and use our gifts"; "This is our family"; "We feel loved and accepted here", and, "We have a purpose when we are a part of Xarts and we feel a part of a bigger story."

There are some keys here that are essential to creating a culture:

- Everyone needs to feel as if they belong.

- Everyone needs to feel accepted and loved.

- Everyone needs to feel they can be part of something bigger than themselves.

- Everyone needs accountability and real relationships.

- Everyone needs to be around people who model a life they want to live themselves.

- Everyone needs to feel that they are in a place with people they can trust.

- Everyone needs to be a part of something in which they are able to contribute.

- Everyone needs to be in a place where they can truly question, search, make mistakes, and still feel the support, love and forgiveness of the team.

These key elements create a missional culture that crosses the ages and gives families glue to be missional together.

Are you committed to finding that "sweet spot" where a culture of mission is created and lived out? I certainly am. What is stopping you?

Paul says in I Corinthians 9: 22: "I have become all things to all men so that by all possible means I might save some".

Is it not our mandate to do whatever it takes to help people find their place in the Kingdom and be transformed?

Time to Collide:

Take some time out to consider the following questions in your own context.

1. Can you think of a time in your ministry or family where the mission has brought people together and caused a collision?

   _____

   _____

2. Can you brainstorm some ways you might be able to help your existing ministries have a stronger strategy of mission?

   _____

   _____

3. Remembering the importance of language, what are some ways you can open up discussion to re-think the current structures to help them to be more missional?

   _____

   _____

4. Look at the keys to create a culture. Choose five ministries in your church and assess these by ticking the keys which the ministries fulfil. Total them up at the bottom to assess what ministries are strongest in creating a culture where children can grow deeper in a holistic way.

   _____

   _____

Keys	Ministry 1	Ministry 2	Ministry 3	Ministry 4	Ministry 5
Everyone needs to feel as if they belong					
Everyone needs to feel accepted and loved					
Everyone needs to feel they can be part of something bigger than themselves					
Everyone needs accountability and real relationships					
Everyone needs to feel they are in a place with people they can trust					

Everyone needs to be a part of something in which they are able to contribute			
Everyone needs to be in a place where they can truly question, search, make mistakes, and still feel the support, love and forgiveness of the team.			
Everyone wants to be around people who model a life they want to live themselves			
Total =			

Chapter 7

Isolation V's Collision: across the generations

The Western Orphans?

We are familiar with orphanages and often place them in developing countries. Our assumption is that they are designed to care for children who do not have parents. We would like to believe that the majority of orphanages are built and manned for the good of the children. It is interesting to read David Tolfree's book, *Roofs and roots: The care of separated children in the developing world.*. He says that studies have shown there are five strong reasons why orphanages have more of a negative effect on children even if they are well run. He says that children in orphanages:

- Lack the opportunity for close relationships with trusted adults.

- Lack the opportunity to learn traditional roles and skills required to live in society.

- Develop a deep sense of dependability, which doesn't help them to become self-reliant and self-directing.

- Lose their sense of family, clanship or tribal identity. They enter adult life without the support of the extended family and community traditions, which hinders their development and assimilation into adulthood. [68]

It is interesting that in a sense orphanages have isolated children from what is really important. For admirable reasons they have missed some very key issues about community and holistic growth. As a result of these findings, there has been a move in Cambodia, and other countries, to help the orphans of the poor stay in their villages with extended families. This is helping them collide with all generations.

"Community based care offers orphaned children the opportunity to maintain a sense of connectedness to their extended family and community,

---

68   Tolfree, D. 1995, *Roofs and roots, Arena, Aldershot, UK, p.142.*

> *Because so much of their life is connected by technology, young people can fail to develop face-to-face people skills*

a vital source of solace and support. The approach allows a greater level of community and child participation and is inherently more sustainable. Finally, as Christians, community based care allows us to impact the entire community for Christ, not just a select group of children being raised in a cloistered environment."[69] While that is an important discovery for the developing world and the truly orphaned poor, why is it not the same for everyone? It has been interesting for me to experience the strength of family in developing countries and the richness of that being displayed in Cambodia. This has been a personal challenge to our family here in Australia as well. I know that in Australia even the government's focus has changed, they now try to keep families together as much as possible and try to support them. The biggest challenges I see to their progress is not only the breakdown of family across western nations but the isolation that is occurring right across this next generation.

We are all still longing for real connection. Yet, the fear for this next western generation is that they are overconnected. This is viewed by many to be a danger.

"Because so much of their life is connected by technology, young people can fail to develop face-to-face people skills. Texting, for instance just doesn't prepare them to interact in real relationship dilemmas. Durable and lasting relationships cannot be reduced to a few words on a screen. And trying to resolve conflict or "breaking up" on a screen is a lazy person's solution. In my opinion, screens are for information - not emotion."[70]

So while there is an over connection regarding the internet, it is done in isolation. I have to ask: Are we walking down the same track as the developing countries' orphanages when, even in a home with everything that whistles and buzzes, the same issues of isolation can occur?

I would say, yes. As a result of isolation we have a generation of young people who suffer greatly from the above issues. It is not just Generation Y kids; it is my generation as well.

69   *Greenfield, C. 2007, The Urban Halo, Authentic Media, USA p.179.*
70   *Elmore, pg 21.*

Connecting the generations is the key to helping these issues.

Let's explore the effects of isolation in the family and institutional Church Structure.

Drop off mentality vs. Integration

A big challenge for the institutional church structure is the 'drop off' mentality. It is not simply a church problem as we find it is very much a part of our society today. It is dangerous to have the attitude of dropping off our children at Day Care as soon as they are born. This is a place where someone else will teach them how to socialize and learn the basics of reading and writing. Then we drop them off to school where they are taught basic principles to get by in life. Then, after school, we drop them off to after-school care or some extra-curricular activity where someone else teaches them other skills. With after-school care sometimes it is merely survival skills they are learning. We even drop them at the TV or computer when they are home to be entertained and taught by that medium. Many families find themselves in a place where they have lost all influence in a child's life because of this "drop-off" mentality.

The church adds to this problem. We drop our children off at a Sunday program to let someone else teach our kids spirituality, while we go to our own Sunday program. Forgive me if I sound very negative about the state of affairs with many families today.

This creates a sense of isolation in families. There is a growing fear of not knowing how to relate to our children. George Barna states that while most Christian parents would love to have some input into their child's lives spiritually, the issue is they don't know how. We have complicated the journey of faith to the point where the average Christian doesn't even know how to live it, let alone model it and share it with those they love the most.

Integration is not easy. It is the long term investment route. It must be intentional and strategic. Families and communities that do have it, have to work hard for that type of integration. It is not something you turn on and off, or try to fit into a time slot. It is every day and all the time.

There have been many times my own family has had to fight for time together and true integration, which gets harder as our children get older. My children and husband understand that we live each day for Christ no matter what happens. Jesus affects the way we respond to each other; the way we handle every situation; the way we talk to others; the way we treat other, and what we do with our time. It is not simply a Sunday thing and it is not something we can't talk about. Rarely a day goes by that we are not challenged, or talking or praying about something. God lives in us and through us. It is the missional life. There are countless times where the moments are a struggle – collision in the most difficult sense – but usually we have found we can make it through. These times help us all to grow a little stronger.

Fighting for integration requires you to be strong about your time together. It means you must create environments where everyone feels safe, loved and appreciated. It always means compromise for everyone at some level. For our family it means setting boundaries on technology, social life and work. We make sure we have quality time together and do things that build us all. It means working hard at finding common ground. It also means doing something with a sense of purpose and value together, so we can all feel that we are achieving something greater than ourselves and creating memories we can all enjoy together.

For our family in particular it requires lots of laughter, adventure, the creative arts and, usually, travel. When we can combine all that while serving God, we are fully integrated. Those times have been some of the best family moments and community moments we have shared. They don't come by accident. We have been very strategic with our time, money and resources to make sure experiences like the above-mentioned have been a priority in our walk with God and each other.

Isolation of faith from our normal day to day lives.

There are others that find they love to be together, do holidays together, sport together, go to the movies together, the beach the park etc. But, they have isolated their faith to a one hour slot on a Sunday morning. So, because they often do this separately, they find it hard to bring it into everyday life.

If we are to understand the missional life we are called to, it is not only about the hour on Sunday but actually about the rest of the week.

A minister once described church as a place where we turn our engine off, and fill up, refuel. This is fine as long as we understand that the true mission of God is when we leave the service, the input, the safe place. We are supposed to turn the engine on when we leave church and begin to be the light in the world for the sake of the Gospel message.

Instead, the institutional church has become the place to find God, and we seem to think that for the rest of the week we are left to our own devices. The missional church happens 24/7. We are the missional church. The family unit is a living breathing church within the community it finds itself in. Together we are meant to be a light to impact the world for Jesus. If every family understood that, we would truly live very differently.

For a Christian, living in upper class suburbia is not as safe as you think. When we first moved into the street, Sam (my son) was going on five. It wasn't long until there was a knock at the door and three children aged seven, nine and eleven wanted to know if Sam could come and play outside. At this stage, he was not able to play out on the road by himself, even though the street was a cul-de-sac and relatively quiet. Sam, being the extrovert that he is, was very unimpressed when I said, "Not today thanks. Sam is too young to play out on the road just yet".

He went into his room to sulk and I went back to the kitchen. I thought that those kids were a little old for Sam, but it was nice for them to ask for him to play. I then began to hear voices coming from Sam's room. The three children had gone to Sam's window and were talking to him. As I crept closer to his room to hear what was being said, (as every nosy mum does), I was horrified to hear them telling Sam to lie to his mum and say he was going out the back to play. They said they would open the side gate and let him out and he could play with them and Mum would never know. I quickly ran to the kitchen and pretended that I was working, with my heart beating

If we are to understand the missional life we are called to, it is not only about the hour on Sunday but actually about the rest of the week

111

hard. I wondered what Sam would do with this situation. What a test of obedience and respect it would be. I knew, of course, that my son would say, "No, thank you" to the children. He'd accept my decision that they were too old for him to play with just yet. I was shocked to see Sam come out of his room, and very guiltlessly say, "Mum, I am just going down the backyard to play. Okay?" And then he ran down the stairs.

My heart sank. My son lied and disobeyed me… And so easily! He was only five. I couldn't believe it. I thought, "What do I do now? Surely he is not going to go through with this deception?"

I snuck down the stairs and into the laundry where I could see them all at the side gate. Sam was on the back veranda stairs. They were all saying, "Come on Sam, your mum will never know? Who really cares? Or maybe just let us in and we will play in your back yard".

I could see Sam listening, hesitating and obviously struggling with this dilemma he had found himself in. At this stage I could not stand it any longer. I walked out of the laundry and very calmly said to Sam, "Go to your room." I told the children at the gate I was very disappointed with their behaviour and that Sam would not be playing with them. I also told them I didn't expect to see them around the place for a while. That was the first experience with the kids down the street.

The youngest was a boy called Blair. He and Sam were both outside boys and loved to ride their bikes, scooters and skateboards. Over the years they did strike up a friendship, by the nature of hanging out on the street and riding all afternoon. It was hard to hinder that relationship. It wasn't long before Blair was in our house regularly and spending most of the school holidays with us.

Being the youngest of four, he was used to being the one who was picked on and bullied. I think he liked being in our house where he was the oldest. Of course he was allowed to go anywhere, at any time, and was often in the street way after dark. He had the latest gadgets and no restrictions of what he could watch. He spoke a language that was not allowed in our house. He knew about things and did things that I would rather my son knew nothing about.

This caused a dilemma. It is one thing to want to be "salt and light in the world" where I was ministering to this type of kid at the church on a daily basis. To have that kind of child come into my home and influence my son, was quite a different story. I felt very passionately that we needed to reach out and be an example of Jesus to those we come into contact with, but I was scared of what this boy would teach my child and how he might influence Sam. There was a strong justification for me to not allow Sam to play with Blair. Let's face it, it would have been the easy option, but something in my spirit knew that this was the faith journey.

Sam was given very strong boundaries and consequences if he broke them. To my surprise, it didn't take long for Blair to become very respectful while in our house. He even stopped pushing Sam to go places where he was not allowed. I thought that Blair would lose interest quickly playing with a kid that had such strict rules but, actually, he respected them. Sam was always home when he was supposed to be and always played where was supposed to. Blair even curbed his language when in our house.

There were times that I knew Sam felt a lot of pressure to play with Blair and do what he wanted to do. Blair was a very lonely little boy, with no other friends and an older brother that bullied him. Sam pretty quickly felt very uncomfortable in their house and chose not to go there. Then the question of sleepovers came and I was happy to have Blair at our house, but was sickened at the thought of Sam staying at his house. When Blair was at our house, he had to go to bed at a time he was not used to. I would take his PSP so he couldn't play it all night and go onto the internet and do whatever he wanted, which he was used to doing. I thought he would never come back, but he did.

I talked to Sam about having a code word that he could use, when he really didn't want to do something, but didn't have the confidence to say no to Blair's face. When they would ask him to do something, Sam would use the code word, I would know to say, "Sam isn't allowed to go". This gave Sam the support he needed to handle peer pressure. While I was really struggling with this relationship, I felt it had to be a learning process for Sam. He had to learn to make the right decisions about what is a real friend. Over the years we took Blair to many of our faith community events, to family picnics and to ten pin bowling. It was his first experience of bowling and he loved it so much he is now part of the local team..

As they moved into High School the age difference became more obvious and they naturally spent less time together. But I remember one time at a street Christmas party, a family up the road starting speaking to me about how wonderful my son is when he is on the street. I was chuffed at that. In the next breath they said, "Man your son has changed Blair's behaviour. That kid was heading nowhere good, and very fast and your son's influence has been amazing. Sam is a great kid". Wow! I had the power to shelter my son and stop that relationship. I could have kept him safe in cotton wool, in a safe home environment, and stunted all the character growth and challenge we had as a family during those years. That story is not over, but the faith journey continues. The isolation of faith from our normal daily lives is a cause for great concern.

Sit and soak vs. engage and participate.

If we want to explore the isolation of families in the institutional church we need to be willing to ask the question, "What do we mainly do at our churches?"

This is a dangerous question and I have found myself in a lot of trouble simply by asking it. Many services I go to are about sitting and soaking. We are very rarely asked to engage and participate. We have created a culture that is so strong that I get a lot of resistance from adults when I ask them to engage and participate. Generations of Christians have been taught to come, sit, give money and do what they are asked when asked. The institution of "Sunday School" has become one of training to sit and soak. Educationalists will tell you that it is the worst format for learning. Yes, there are some things you need to simply sit and process through but, unless they are ultimately put into practice at some point, you will eventually lose any kind of learning that went on in the first place.

When an institution is largely functioning on the principal of sit and soak, then it is like turning the Titanic: a seemingly impossible task. I believe the reason we are seeing many Churches on the dying edge, is that there are some things that simply need to die before new growth can occur.

On the other hand I have seen God do what would seem impossible, when a group of fifty people who had been in the institutional church their whole lives, were called to do something new in their community. God has transformed these people's perceptions of what is means to be a missional community. They have changed everything, including their language, to be a missional and true community.

I have had one older distinguished lady say to me a number of times over the past few years, "I have been sitting in a pew all my life and followed Jesus, but never in my whole life have I felt so alive and excited about serving Him, since we started this community. I have walked away from all that I knew was church and I would never have thought that in my sixties I could be so excited about serving God as I am today, being a part of this community of Christians we call ICentral316".

What a difference engaging and participating can make in the lives of people of any age.

If you look at the UK, and what is happening with the movement of "Fresh Expressions" we see that people are being taken out of the institutional system to be specifically trained for the very purpose of engaging and participating in the community God calls them to. John Gray

> *The institution of "Sunday School" has become one of training to sit and soak. Educationalists will tell you that it is the worst format for learning*

says, "We call them "pioneer ministers" and they are being trained up to learn that they need to die to live. They have to be willing to die to what church means to them and then something new grows (John 12:24)."[71]

Lucy Moore's "Messy church" model is engaging families and people all over England and beyond. People come back to faith in an environment in which, instead of being asked to sit and soak, they are encouraged to engage and participate. It is a simple yet effective model of church community that is releasing new life into churches all over England.

"Participation is about inviting everyone to engage with different elements of the service in a way that makes them comfortable but sometimes gently takes them out of that comfort zone to a place of challenge."[72]

71   Gray, John 2009, from Fresh Expressions in the UK, Arrow Conference Speaker, Melbourne.
72   Moore, L. 2010, All age Worship, The bible reading fellowship, UK, p.100.

It is one of many models that is asking the question, "How can we empower families and people to find Christ in a relevant and life giving way; a way that gets them moving and acting on their faith and which is appropriate and engaging for all ages?"

Stop the isolation and silos and start to collide!

1. I believe there is a better chance for transformation when we collide all these elements of the faith journey, rather than live them in isolation.

2. I also believe that we have a better chance of transformation when we combine colliding across the generations at the same time as colliding the elements.

Exploring the benefits of Collision for all the generations in a faith community.

The key question is: What can we do together that we can't do apart?

This question has been asked in our faith community. As a result we have created, across the generations, collisions that have been not only community building but also character building, and have encouraged us to all grow more deeply with Christ at the same time.

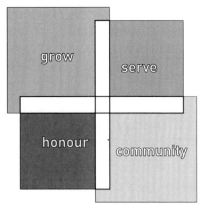

When it comes to colliding with all the generations across the four elements, it is worth exploring and it is easier than it seems.

My Cup overflows: a story of an integrated collision across the generations.

"It is amazing how much can come from one cup," she says at the end of a two-day retreat where woman aged from thirty three to seventy three gathered together with their favourite cup. It is often in the simple things we see the most precious collisions. You may say, "It's a no-brainer, getting

116

a group of woman in the same room and getting them talking", but there is something special when God turns up.

The environment was created: a nice hideaway retreat house, a warm fire, a cosy bed, a spa and pool, and plenty of bushland to discover. For many it was an opportunity to be away from being "mummy" and "wife", or someone's "partner". A place where going to bed and getting up was your call. Everyone brought a meal. The food was certainly a highlight over the weekend and each meal seemed to top the next. It looks like a recipe book will come from the weekend as many appreciated someone else's creations.

After each meal, we would simply use the favourite cup we brought, and one lady led the group with a thought each meal around our cup. We meditated on: the empty cup, the open cup, the broken cup, the chipped cup and the cup of blessing. Sometimes, hours later, we would still be there, talking, listening, crying and laughing together. It took some ladies all weekend to speak. Others didn't stop from the moment we got there. Either way it was okay. Across the generations we shared about marriage, struggles, parenting, the struggle to see God and the beauty of when He shows Himself. It was beautiful to see the wisdom of those who have walked with him for fifty years as they shared with those who have just begun the journey. And sometimes the younger ones taught those who had been on the journey for a long time, a different way to see things.

There was acceptance and love for those who still don't believe and compassion was shown when some shared they wanted to give up all together. It was all there colliding together. We will never know all of what God was doing in our midst, but we all walked away strengthened by the time we spent there. We were satisfied and challenged to move forward in our faith, relationships and love for each other.

Creating environments where the generations can collide can sometimes be as simple as integrating good food, good space, a safe place to share and a lot of time.

A created space of worship across the generations.

We have worked hard to find spaces and elements of worship that work across the generations. We have found that drama, music, food, laughter,

physical challenges, multimedia, addressing everyday issues and Godly values are all places where age is not an issue and common ground is found. When we meet all together for our worship celebrations all those elements help us to worship together. We address a specific Godly value each month and have found the resources of *www.252basics.org* a great way to start the process. We have created a drama from that material that has characters right across the generations. We find Grandpa in the shed (the place to escape and reflect) and Nana May in the kitchen (the heartbeat of the home). The lounge is the place where the ages meet and interact. It is a place where you will find sisters and brothers clashing; dad trying to make sense of it all; the crazy neighbour always butting in, and friends drop over to add their two cents. The scene is set to address many daily issues, and then to have a space to look at what God has to say about it. We meet around tables for prayer and discussions and challenges where the ages engage together, and the teaching is dispersed through interactive presentations and music and multimedia.

All in all it is a joy to be together, young and old, growing and worshipping together and spurring each other on the journey.

A way to reach out to others, up to God and in to each other all at the same time.

This Easter we went on the journey together through the Easter story. Easter is a time when people will go to a church. This year they walked through the whole experience from the last supper through to the resurrection. We met in people's houses, and moved from house to house. As a faith community we spent the weekend of Easter together. We had some non-Christians join us. It was a rich experience of eating together, partying together, crying together, and witnessing the last days of Jesus re-enacted.

We started with the last supper at someone's house. At the end of the meal, there was some social time. Then the last supper was re-enacted and we all peered in as we sat at the table and took the last supper as Jesus served it up. Then we went to someone else's house in a convoy of cars. In the garden the Gethsemane scene was re-enacted. Jesus was taken away by guards and we were led by woman watching to somewhere else. We moved to a place where there was a fire and while we were all warming our hands, Peter came and the denial was re-enacted. It was a powerful time when the cock crowed three times and Peter left in a panic. We spent the rest of the night around the fire – all ages, having supper – and people left when they wanted to.

As they were leaving everyone was given an invitation to someone's house for breakfast and asked to wear black. At breakfast, all ages together went through the stages of Jesus' death in an interactive way. We prayed together. Then we met at the church for the resurrection celebration. It was done with music and drama and had very powerful accounts of people who had met Jesus and the impact that He had had on them.

We finished with a party feel and the people were given some colour to add to their black as a reminder of the celebration of new life in Him.

This was another way that we were able to reach in to each other and share Easter together across the ages. Our community invited people to certain aspects or to all of the weekend, as it was free for anyone to come. God was truly honoured and worshipped that Easter weekend. It was a collision worth all the effort, as the load was shared about amongst many of our faith community members and they all felt they could play a part.

The script of the Easter Experience is free to download and use from www.collide.net.au.

Benefits of Colliding across the ages:

- There is usually less work because it is spread among many.

- There is usually less programming and therefore less stress on everybody.

- There is such a breadth of gifts and resources among the whole community that make the collisions so interesting.

- There is less formal structure to the events, and more informal relational structure, which allows for ease for all leading.

- There is always food involved and that is a great thing.

- When there is a mentality that we come together to serve and give, there is always an ample number of people to do the tasks. It is a joy to see the atmosphere that is created when we all come to be a part of it, rather than just sit and soak it up.

- It is harder to blame, or complain, when we are all involved in the process.

- Although time is so precious, I never feel as if getting together it is a waste of time. We all give and get something from it.

Time to Collide:

Take some time out to consider the following questions in your own context.

1. What would Christmas dinner be without all the parts of your extended family? Think about what you are missing when your faith community is in different parts of the church and never able to interact together.

_____

_____

_____

_____

2. In your community, what can you do together that you cannot do apart?

_____

_____

_____

_____

3. In your family, how much easier is it to maintain the house if you all do a part of the job? Isn't that what the body concept is all about? (I Cor 12) What can you empower someone else to do?

_____

_____

_____

_____

_____

4. Can you see how having a discussion group about certain issues across the ages could be so much more interesting?

_____

_____

_____

_____

_____

Chapter 8

Creating environments for collision across the generations

"Environments are vital - alive. They are not inanimate – dead. When places encourage community to emerge spontaneously, they have motion, emotion, and a living spirit. The goal is not to manufacture community. Neither is the goal to build programs. The hope is to watch living community emerge naturally and collaborate with its environment in helpful, healthy ways."[73]

Menconi believes strongly that the issue of being together across the generations is paramount. He states "Over the next several decades, intergenerational churches have great potential to impact individual lives and transform society. The degree to which

> *Over the next several decades, intergenerational churches have great potential to impact individual lives and transform society*

churches are successful in achieving effective intergenerational ministry will determine the effectiveness of their overall ministries."[74]

To know me is to love me

"If you've gotten anything at all out of following Christ, if his love has made any difference in your life, if being in a community of the Spirit means anything to you, if you have a heart, if you care — then do me a favor: Agree with each other, love each other, be deep-spirited friends. Don't push your way to the front; don't sweet-talk your way to the top. Put yourself aside, and help others get ahead. Don't be obsessed with getting your own advantage. Forget yourselves long enough to lend a helping hand (Philippians 2:1-4; The Message Bible)."

One of the challenges with creating collisions across the generations is learning to accept and understand our differences. We grow in maturity

---

73   *Meyers, p.171.*

74   *Menconi, Peter 2010, "The Intergenerational Church; Understanding Congregations from WW11 to* www.com*, Mt Sage Publishing, Littleton, CO, pg 21*

when we can work alongside and respect each other's differences. It would be a boring world if we were all the same, but it is amazing how uncompromising we can be when we have to work with someone who is different from us. This is an age-old issue which I believe becomes easier when we understand that God needs to reframe our thinking. On our own we just can't do it.

"If church is about loving God and loving each other and transforming the world in partnership with Him and with each other, can we achieve that best by splitting up or by learning to live together? If I cannot learn to cope with praying in church with a slightly smelly 80 year old, a 15 year old who is cleverer than I am, a toddler who wriggles, or a woman who won't stop weeping, what hope do I have of loving people outside the Church?".[75]

When God birthed our new faith community in 2005 we were faced very quickly with issues that could have destroyed us or could make us stronger. We collided very quickly on a number of issues, in a very messy way that was not comfortable for anyone. But, I say with great humility that God was teaching us all about love, forgiveness and acceptance.

We wanted to create a new kind of faith community; a new environment. For a long time, it did feel as if we were walking into the desert like the Israelites. As one of the leaders of this community, I was quickly surprised by how many people wanted to "go back to Egypt". I mean that they wanted to go back to what was familiar, when it got a little unknown and unclear for their liking. I was surprised how simple it was to revert to what we knew, rather than explore new territory.

If church is about loving God and loving each other and transforming the world in partnership with Him and with each other, can we achieve that best by splitting up or by learning to live together?

I remember struggling with the older people in our community as they wanted to have a traditional Sunday service that would be familiar and comfortable. There was a group of us who were very strong about not wanting this type of service. We wanted to be free to explore how

---

75   Moore, p.52.

we could do something different. It could have been the end of us very early on, as a community, if we didn't love and appreciate the needs and differences of the generations.

I thought the older people were doing the wrong thing, but our love for each other, and hopefully wisdom and empathy, prevailed and we allowed elements to happen even when we didn't feel comfortable with them. That was right across the board. There was understanding and grace from both sides and, if I am honest, there was a constant fight within me to not say how wrong I felt they were.

Still today there is a strong group that meets on Sunday mornings and for them it has been their strength; it is their life group. Others of us meet in homes for our life groups. But we all appreciate and love each other and just about everything else we do is together across the generations. I believe we are all stronger because we showed grace and acceptance even when we did not understand or agree. It has also strengthened our time together across the generations, as the majority of the time we are all together in ministry and serving the community in our intergenerational celebrations. As a community we love to meet and share with each other.

There has to be some give and take. There has to be a lot of love and acceptance to successfully collide with the generations. In the church at large, we too often find that lack of acceptance and love leads to hurt and misunderstanding, resulting in division and people going their separate ways.

Tim Elmore sets out a clear table of differences and diversity that are to be celebrated rather than becoming issues that divide us. [76] I think there is something positive we can learn from all the generations if we are open to each other.

---

76   *Elmore, p.138,*

	Builders	Boomers	Generation x (Busters)	Generation Y
View of life	I am grateful for it	I will conquer it	I will endure it	I will change the world
Work	I see work as a duty and a privilege	I live to work	I work to live	I work to make a difference
Relation-ships	I am loyal, but private Significant	I network to get ahead, Useful	Friends are my family Caring and Central	I'm connected globally
Family	Close family	Dispersed family	Latchkey kids	Looser family definitions
Marriage Patterns	Married once	Divorced and remarried	Single parent	Desire lifelong partner but cautious
High Tech	Slide rule	Calculator, TV	Computers	Smart phone
Tech-nology	Hope to outlive it	Master it	Enjoy it	Employ it
Money	Save it now	Buy it now	Want it now	Get it now
View of Self	I'm humble, resourceful	I am the centre	I'm lonely and need community	I play a role on a team
Attitude to Authority	Endure them	Replace them	Ignore them	Choose them
Schedules	Mellow	Frantic	Aimless	Volatile
Market	Goods	Services	Experiences	Transform-ation
View of the future	Seek to stabilize	Create it	Hopeless	Optimistic
Life Paradigm	Be grateful you have a job	You owe me	Relate to me	Life is a cafeteria

The challenge is learning to value each other's perspective and differences and to eventually reach the point where we can celebrate them.

In the faith community I belong to I see this time and time again. One Sunday a month we meet together for breakfast. (We call it "Brekky Central"). The joy of sharing food can never be underestimated, especially when you have wonderful cooks in the community who cook the most amazing eggs. I remember one of our people ringing me to ask that we save her some eggs, as she didn't want to miss out. But, other than the food, this time is largely to connect and share stories together as a community. I overheard one young mother, who has not had a very positive relationship with her own mother, share that she loves to hear our older ladies sharing about anything. She says she never tires of hearing them speak, as they speak with such wisdom, gentleness and love.

She is not alone in this; many of us have come to respect the sages around us who have an honoured voice in our community. We must create environments where this can occur. This is a very powerful spiritual act of worship together across the ages. As a parent I long for someone to speak into the lives of our own children. In our community our children have many grandparents, aunties and uncles, big brothers and little sisters. I love to hear the older youth say things that I know my children will listen to. I know that they would not be so impacted if these things were coming from me. I have watched so many people of all ages speak into each other's lives and know that it has have been transformational. I hope that I have been able to give back to other families as they have given to mine. It must run both ways.

We participated in one very powerful forum where we brought all the ages together to ask the question, "What is the gift we bring to the other generations and what do we value about those who are not in our generation?"

We were put into age groups to discuss those two aspects of the question, and a spokesperson for each group shared the thoughts of that group to the others. We listened as every age group was addressed and affirmed.

Imagine a twelve year old speaking to a sixty year old about what their age group valued about them and vice versa. It was very powerful for all involved. It required listening and speaking intentionally into other's lives. We were all encouraged and affected deeply, but interestingly enough it was the top and bottom end of the age spectrum that was most affected. The builders and the iY Generation were each given a voice and were respected. This can only happen when we are willing to get to know each other and appreciate each other's perspectives. To know me is to love me.

It takes time

In ancient Jewish culture children participated in seven festivals every year. These festivals included food, dancing, laughter, stories and learning. Some of them would last seven to ten days. Everyone would be together, much like us when we celebrate Easter and Christmas. They would have been very rich in their faith development and their sense of being a part of a greater story. The challenge for us today is to be strategic about creating these environments across the generations. It takes time and effort and this seems to overwhelm people.

Parents and families say they want this environment, but somehow need the motivation to make it a priority. The faith community can be a powerful place where we create an environment where people, families, of all ages can play together. Eighty percent of parents want more information about how to improve their relationships with their children, yet fear of criticism acts as a barrier to parents asking for support and information.[77] We often think that running a course is the only way to bridge these gaps.

My childhood is filled with amazing memories and I am thankful that my parents took time to make sure I was in environments that were life-giving. As a whole Christian community, we would go on bike riding camps and waterskiing camps two to four times a year. We would be dirty and grimy and simply all hang out together. One minute the minister would be jumping in the mud with us and then the next day he would be sharing communion around the fire. All the ages were together: living, laughing, loving, playing and growing together. Different ages, different personalities. Sometimes conflicts would arise as tent walls are very thin, but mostly life was grand on these weekends. They are anchor points in my childhood that gave me a strong foundation of who I wanted to be and how I wanted to live. We have been very strategic in creating these anchor points for our own children.

---

77   *Australian Childhood foundation, March 2005.*

Sometimes the best collisions are the easiest to create, but they do take time. Hopefully this is deemed time well spent, not time people feel is a hassle. Pack a tent, some clothes, food and find a remote place to all hang out together for some time and see what collisions occur.

> *Family ministry is not just a ministry to families and ministry for families, but also a ministry with and in families. We want to encourage more opportunities for our families to experience life in Christ together*

"Family ministry is a way to bring the generations together. We are recognising that by dividing our ministries exclusively by ages and stages we contribute to the fragmentation of families. Family ministry is not just a ministry to families and ministry for families, but also a ministry with and in families. We want to encourage more opportunities for our families to experience life in Christ together."[78]

Forging New paths is not easy

It is one thing to be unhappy with the state of affairs and say we need to do something; we need to see change. It is entirely another thing to forge new paths. It is important to desire to be deeply rooted in Christ, yet another to actually live it. The Lord said the road would be narrow.

> *"But small is the gate and narrow the road that leads to life, and only a few find it"*
>
> (Matthew 7:14).

In Acts 10-11, Peter was eating the food he had grown up with all his life, for he was taught that he should never eat certain foods. Imagine the internal struggle for Peter to re-think what God was asking him to do when God asked him to eat food that was forbidden? (Acts 10:14-15). Here we see a great example of a godly man misunderstanding God's big picture, although he was taught by the institutional church of the time. God was reframing his thinking and, for Peter, to forge new paths was not easy. We have to be willing to walk into new places and think about things from a different perspective, even if it means for a while you really don't understand or feel uncomfortable.

---

78   Allen, Holly 2010, *Director of children and family ministry at John Brown University, Children's Ministry.com.*

> *You sink the operation if you go into it thinking you already know what it is going to look like*

I heard someone say once, "We all love a drama, until it is happening to us." I think about that in regards to movies. The movies I most love are the ones where transformation has occurred within the most challenging of circumstances. And yet, when colliding together becomes hard or challenging, we question if we have gone down the right track.

"You sink the operation if you go into it thinking you already know what it is going to look like."[79]

I believe it takes getting out of your normal situation to free your mind for new things. Under the covering of Freshhope ministries we have launched a new ministry called "Collide" in Australia. One of its expressions is a two day retreat, away from the busyness of life. Anyone, any group, any family combination, any faith community can come along and take time out together to reframe. It is a start. During this weekend we have created environments where all ages can collide spiritually, emotionally, socially, physically and intellectually together. It is a holistic, experiential weekend where people of all ages can have space to re-think out of actual experiences and environments created for them. I am convinced that to forge new paths we sometimes need what I call a "jump start of the heart". At the end of that time there is a challenge to participants to process. They must work through the key principles of what a collision might look like for them in their home, faith community and the local community in which they live and are called to be the light of the world.

We continue to encourage everyone to share stories about what a collision looks like; to spur each other to re-think and forge new paths. Here are some of those stories.

I like leaves too! Posted by Adam, 30 August (2011)
About 5 months ago I was having a chat over morning tea with Alice, an older lady from my church. During the conversation I mentioned that my son Jake (6) really liked collecting interesting leaves.

---

79   *Gray, John 2009, Arrow Conference, Melbourne.*

About one month later, Alice excitedly approached me on a Sunday morning asking whether Jake was here today. Before I pointed her in the right direction, I asked why she was so excited to know if he was around. She opened her handbag and pulled out a tiny photo album. Flicking through the pages she showed me a vast collection of different and unique leaves that she had gone out and collected from her garden. She had put one leaf into each photo sleeve and written a little caption about the leaf. She wanted to give it to Jake as a gift.

I had forgotten about our leaf collecting conversation, but she hadn't. I was unaware that Alice was into botanical things. But our little conversation had sparked in her a desire to connect. She saw an opportunity to share something in common with my son; nothing spiritual, just a chance to develop a friendship with someone much younger than herself.

I was (and am still) blown away by this. I am overwhelmed that someone would take such great time to invest into a relationship with someone so much younger, just for the sake of making a friend.

Jake has this little album in a special place in his room. And when he finds a new and interesting leaf, he puts it in the back of the album, and every few weeks now I see Alice and Jake chatting together on a Sunday morning, showing each other new things each of them have collected.

There is much I can learn from the actions of Alice.

Men Collide and become Stronger. Posted by Tim, 6 September (2011)
Fathers' Day, for some, holds great memories, for others, a missing part of a childhood or a pain that cannot be explained in words.

We decided as a Community of Believers to spend two days away from distractions to rest, relax, and recharge, but what happened was a series of collisions. Our youngest camper was 4 years old, our oldest in his 50s, and that weekend around 30 of us spent time together, playing cricket, soccer, cooking, swimming, or resettling with tents that seemed to have no logical way to assemble.

Some collisions were funny to be a part of - "Who forgot the egg flipper?", "Did you bring your child's spare clothes?", "How do you play this game where you throw a Nerf Ball into the air at night and hope that it hits someone?....(Thud)... oh now I get it... ouch".

But the more important collisions were the ones where we had time to share stories, ideas, struggles, and triumphs in life. Parenting tips, or simple tips on all kinds of things from camping and tent assembly, to" how do we get out of here?"

This was a positive collision experience. I would encourage others to spend some time away, and look for the collision points that help build relationships. Others personally have blessed me because of this experience.

It will BE different for everyone

Intergenerational ministry is context-specific and should be customized to fit a particular church's history, culture, location, staff, and vision. It is not "one size fits all." Churches that have been successful started with what they were already doing well in one of the ministries of the church, and then asked, "Since this is already good (or even great), what would it take to move to the next level and use this to become intergenerational?" Identify key influencers in the congregation who already have an intergenerational mindset and enlist their help[80].

I know the biggest barriers for truly colliding has been that people want a formula they can implement, or a model they can easily follow. The challenge is that to be intergenerational, it requires a mindset rather than a strategy. You need to re-think the way you do life. I have tried to show by the many examples in this book that it is worth the journey, even though it will look different for everyone.

> *Intergenerational ministry is context-specific and should be customized to fit a particular church's history, culture, location, staff, and vision. It is not "one size fits all"*

Part of the importance of sharing the stories is to celebrate the differences. That is where we find the beauty. As stated before, I love to go to the movies. I love to escape into an adventure and I especially love the true stories. They are all different and unique. They are

80   Snailum, Brenda, 2010, Promoting Intergenerational Youth Ministry Within Existing Evangelical Church Congregations: What Have We Learned?, Talbot Theological Seminary, Fall Issue.

often filled with twists and turns, hardships and celebrations. People are rarely the same at the end of the story. Imagine how boring it would be if every movie, every story was the same. There's nothing worse than movies that are written to a formula. The classic romance story can get boring after a while. Boy meets girl, they fall in love, something happens to stretch that love, they push through and they live happily ever after. But even within that general formula, there is individuality, challenges and things that make their story look different. We need to stop looking for a formula or an easy five step plan.

The key is to start where you are at and begin to bring together a group of people that have a similar mindset. Once you have that, you can ask: What could a collision look like in our context and location, with the people that God has placed in our midst?

Think outside the box

To truly create environments where the generations can collide, you will need to be thinking far wider than a Sunday morning worship service. Hopefully this book has given you many contexts in which collisions can occur. We really need to step outside of the box that we find ourselves in when we have been doing something for a long time. It happens to all of us.

Every time I read the gospels I am re-shocked into realizing how much Jesus lived outside the box. What Jesus said and did offended people regularly.

> One of the religious scholars spoke up: "Teacher, do you realize that in saying these things you're insulting us?
> (Luke 11:45; MSG).

He shook up much of the way they lived, served and worshipped God. I do not want to offend people or shake up everything we do in Christendom, but I do want to see this generation rooted deeply in Christ. I want to be faithful in whatever that takes, for the sake of children and their families. I know that you feel the same. To do this we will need to think outside the box; to re-frame what we think it means to be the missional church to the world. Once we have worked this through, I believe it will mean you will have to think differently about how we minister and "do" Church. I know this because it has happened to our community. And for us, after experiencing glimpses of true community, we just cannot go back to Egypt. Are you ready to think outside the box?

Where do you start?

Do not try to reinvent everything at once. Start small and avoid big sweeping program changes, particularly before there is adequate ownership of the vision on the part of all stakeholders. Celebrate little wins. Tell stories of success to encourage the congregation and build momentum.[81]

The key is taking a "baby" step in being collaborative in creating environments where the generations can collide. It should be an environment that is holistic in structure and that creates true community for those involved. The great thing about new paths is that the possibilities are endless. The scary thing about new paths is that the possibilities are endless. You may be thinking the book is ending and you still don't have the four step plan to make this work. That's because there is no four step plan. There are some important principles which can help you re-think, and then you need the willingness to step out and see where the journey takes you. I have simply tried to show the need and the benefits of giving it a go.

---

81   Snailum, Brenda,2010, *Promoting Intergenerational Youth Ministry Within Existing Evangelical Church Congregations: What Have We Learned?, Talbot Theological Seminary, Fall Issue.*

Time to Collide:

Take some time out to consider the following questions in your own context.

1. How well do you understand the generations and their differences?

_____

_____

_____

2. Read the Gospels again and answer the following questions:

A. What does it mean to be the "Church" to the world you live in?

_____

_____

_____

B. Who is the church and what should it look like today in Australia?

_____

_____

_____

C. If you were to place your ministry on a continuum between intergenerational and isolation, where would you fall? What about your church as a whole?

_____

_____

_____

Some great books I would recommend are:

- Elmore, Tim 2010, Generation iY – Our Last Chance to Save Their Future, Poet Gardener Publishing, USA.

- Grose, Michael 2005, XYZ – The New Rules of Generational Warfare, Random House, Australia.

- Kinnaman, David 2011, You lost me – why young Christians are leaving Church, Baker Books, USA.

- McQueen, Michael 2011, The new rules of Engagement, Nexen Group, Australia.

What Next?

1. Work with a team or other ministry leaders to discuss what's next.

2. Take some time to dream about what a collision could look like in your community

3. Start small and work with people who are keen to try something new.

4. Share the stories of what has happened to widen the circle of people "buying in" (other owning it) and interest.

5. Do it again

Chapter 9

Tell the stories.

The thing with "collisions, is that the focus needs to be on the journey and not the destination. We are so caught up on markers for success – measures of validity, success or failure – that they can get in the way of what we are called to be a part of. I am speaking to myself as I write this. I can be a driven person.

creating environments
where generations can collide

I want to be able to evaluate myself as someone who has run a good race and can look back and feel life was worth it all.

We must be careful what we measure, as God's timing and view is so different to ours. Imagine if Joseph looked back on his life while he was in jail. He would say, "So I must have really let you down God. I didn't fulfil your plan at all. I am a waste of space". There must be many who have felt like that. I have had many of those days. Just as well this is His story and not ours; His collisions, not ours, and His purpose, not ours.

But along the journey, if you see a story worth sharing, you must stop and share it. This is what keeps us going. I love a good story and I am sure you do too. When I am weary and tired and need a good story I escape to movies and books.

This chapter is full of stories of collisions that have been created across the generations. Even though the story has not ended we have caught a glimpse of why it is valuable to collide whenever we can.

My Story

When we choose to collide it may be such an abrupt experience that it changes everything. The question is, are you truly open to collide? Let me share a bit of my story. In 2003 I had been in ministry for fifteen years. I knew that I was called to make a difference for children in Australia. I was a children's pastor in a large church. The children's ministry was thriving and very much the growing edge of the church. The teams were growing. It was a privilege to watch children and leaders being transformed and finding purpose and joy in God and in serving Him. My children loved being a part of church and the larger family. What a wonderful stage in ministry!

At that time our children were younger: Sam was seven, Georgia four. I was passionate about the fact that as a parent I was a key influencer for my children and their spirituality. I have always believed that we are meant to live the Christian life in community not only with our children, but with a wider community, spanning many generations. I began to ask, "What could that look like? How can I strategically create environments where there can be shared experiences of worship and celebration, with *all* the generations together?" I was convinced we could do more together than we currently were doing. So we began to create an intergenerational worship experience.

A dream, a revelation was forming.

As I began to search for answers, I stumbled upon a ministry at Northpoint Community Church, led by pastor Reggie Joiner, and a team of people who were further down the track following a similar dream. When I walked into Kidstuf for the very first time it felt as if I was in heaven. Reggie Joiner says in his book, *Orange*, that two combined influences make a greater impact than just two influences, and that's what they were modelling at Kidstuf. (www.kidstuf.org)

When I returned home, I knew that things would never be the same. I knew that God was calling me to explore what a similar dream might look like in the Australian context, in my home, in my community!

As I began to talk and dream, it became very apparent that this was going to cost me my current ministry position. It was going to test my integrity, my confidence, my inner strength, my leadership, and maybe even my extended family; everything but my immediate family. To share a dream is a scary thing; to lead in the dark is even scarier. To create the path as you walk it is certainly edgy. Oh please, can't someone else do it? This was way too hard!

In 2005, we began to meet as a small community and dare to dream of what it might look like to be a truly intergenerational community of light and hope. But that had to happen within us first. Nothing was clear, except the desire to be in God's will, to grow as families, and to be lights within a wider community of people who are lost without an eternal hope. Within a few years, a dead building had been brought to life and transformed. A dead manse had been revived to become a house of laughter with children growing in Christ and finding their giftings. An elderly group of people had been empowered to serve in new and exciting ways. A group of children were experiencing first hand that God had gifted them and that they were able to actively live their faith and share it with others. They were now children who were actively engaged as opposed to sitting and learning from a teacher.

One of the biggest challenges was for parents to be honest and admit that they really would rather have someone else look after their children so that they could be free to worship and serve in ways that solely suited them. The families that have stayed have relearned the joy of being together. They have been challenged to disciple their children by being present and active, and by modeling a life that is Christ-centred. This has been a personal challenge to us all, but wonderful when we truly get to do it together.

We have discovered that on the journey of faith, there are no age limits, no prerequisites and no restrictions, just an open heart and a desire to draw near to Him. So much can be gained when we do that together; across the ages, sharing what God is doing in us. We then all see life from the different perspectives represented.

Recently, my family made a decision to spend some strategic time away together. We enjoyed discovering the beautiful country of Australia, but mostly we simply enjoyed being together. We desired for God to be the centre of our life together, whether working or on holidays. It was about seeing life through God's lens.

As we spent time together in close proximity, we had to be a team in setting up and taking down the campervan. We had little worldly distractions and had quality time together. This brought an intimacy I had never experienced in our family, although I always considered us to be a close. There was no way we could have planned or prepared for the learning that God had for us, because it happened as we did life together. We discovered Him over and over again in nature and His creation. We walked through the life of Christ together and talked, shared and prayed from everyone's perspective about what God was teaching us as we read though the book of Mark together and on into Acts. Sometimes it was a chore, sometimes it was a joy, but it was always valuable, because God was doing something at all times.

I felt as though God gave me a glimpse of what He designed the family to be: a strong and safe place from which to venture out. And, a place where the journey together is more valuable than the individual journeys we all went on.

When the seduction of this world is strong for even the most committed of Christians, it is hard to be a light in the darkness. It is so easy to be snuffed out by all that bombards our families today. In the light of this reality, I believe there is strength in a community. It is a place where families journey through life together and support each other during these times. It is not only vital for our children but for the adults as well.

There is great joy for me when I see that within a created experience, a grandmother can share with tears how she is struggling with watching her grandchildren suffering and not know what to do. As she does so a little girl aged seven spontaneously stands up, walks over to her, places her hand on her and begins to pray.

We have seen created environments where a seventy two year old is able stand up in front of twenty five children who have been abused and share his memories of working hard as a teenager, and the value of education. You could hear a pin drop as they all hung onto every word. I have been challenged when, on a family mission trip to Cambodia, my nine year old didn't hesitate to play with snotty-nosed, bare-bottomed children, while I found myself retreating into the bus.

It can happen in the simplicity of a small group experience, or in the complex planning of an overseas mission trip, but it is about being strategic in creating environments where all ages can work, grow and draw nearer to God *together*. Then we are creating a Godly collision and I say bring it on!

In 2011 we launched a new ministry called "Collide". My husband and I are being empowered to create retreats where the generations can collide over a weekend experience. We aim to create dynamic events to help all ages collide together. We hope that this exchange of energy will be a catalyst for personal growth and transformation both within families and within our Christian communities and beyond.

Bash camp

Once a year we create an environment where all the generations can collide in a week long family experience for abused children called, Southern Cross Kids' Camp. This week is for the children, but the staff and team is made up of grandmas, grandpas, aunties, uncles, cousins and children. The only generation not represented is the baby to age seven years group. We create a safe and loving environment where one child and one mentor spend a week together playing, being, experiencing new things and learning about how much God loves them.

The thirty minute bus trip to camp this year was spent by one boy saying that this was "bash camp". He said he was going to bash everyone he met and that everyone would know who he was and that he was to be feared. We knew that God was going to have to help us here, for the week was going to be a hard one. This boy was a good-sized eleven year old with bright red hair and freckles. Without stereotyping him, not one leader doubted that this could be "bash camp" as we headed for the campsite.

There was a text message sent ahead of the bus to the camp to pray, because there were some tough campers on board and we really needed God to help us that week. All forty leaders prayed together for the children by name. They dedicated all the mentors to God, believing that He had it all under control.

As John got off the bus he was connected with his mentor, who was a new to the role, but strong and calm. They spent the afternoon bonding and, to be honest, this child was a beautiful child most of the week. He was gentle, involved, happy, talkative and not one child was bashed all camp. I have been doing these camps for ten years now, so it didn't surprise me that this was the case as I have seen God work in amazing ways. I have also come to know that there is power in creating an environment where youth, children, adults and grandparents can all work together. The safety and security of each child there can really make a difference.

John was up on stage on the last night dancing to a rap song with his mentor and he was alive and magical.

Camp came to a close five days later and we all got on the bus to come home. At the church where the children meet their parents and carers they present a concert. John was up there singing and doing all the actions to the songs with a smile on his face. As we were all saying goodbye, his carer came to get me and said that John was crying around the back of the building. I needed to come and help. We found John crying like a baby. He said that his parents thought he had done something wrong. He was heart-broken. We said we would speak to his parents and sort it all out. When we approached the parents I explained that John felt he was in trouble and they simply looked bewildered. They tried to explain that when they saw him they simply asked, "What happened to you at camp?" While he thought he was in trouble and ran away, they explained that they were literally saying, "What happened at camp", because they did not recognize him. They couldn't believe the change from the child they put on the bus five days earlier. They literally did not recognize him. He had transformed so much that they were in shock!

The power of a created environment that allows abused, angry children to experience God's love can truly make a difference in five days.

A few short hours can change a perspective

It is amazing what you can do with a few sticks, old materials and some newspaper and glue. For two hours a hundred of us – all ages – ventured into the bush to be led in a simulation game about poverty. We were quickly rounded into family groupings of seven to eight people. There had to be a cross section of all ages in each group.

We were taught in five minutes how to make a paper bag out of newspapers and a glue stick. We were told that we had to make as many as possible. As a family group we were given a mat in the bush, which was our home, and if we hadn't made enough money before the whistle blew the landlord would deal with us. It was amazing how quickly the tension and panic set in for us all.

We all worked so hard, yet we could hardly make our quota of bags for each day. Every person was needed and as the game went on, tragedy struck each family in different ways. The landlord would come and take your money, your children, your house, and your resources. If you didn't take the opportunity to send your children to school, you lost them through sickness or another calamity. Very quickly you caught a glimpse of what it might be like to simply try to survive under the poverty line. Some families were sent "under the bridge", which was like being sent into a form of slavery.

I have to admit that when my daughter was sent to another family to be married, I cried. The other time I cried was when there was health training that we didn't attend because that meant stopping making our bags and then we lost another child to sickness. It was not that I was crying about losing a child, because I knew it was only a game. It had a very real impact on me. It made me realize that when we go to other countries and think we are helping by training and offering education, that it is often a big pressure for them to stop working to take the opportunity.

Of course the education is important, but I realized for the first time what great expense it was for to them to come to the training. The experience impacted everyone in different ways and took many of us hours to de-brief. For different age groupings the impact was different and it was great to hear from each other. In the end it was amazing how just a few hours in the right environment could make such a huge impact on so many people of all ages.

Simulations like this and others can be found on the TEAR website[82]. Feel free to download and run them yourself.

---

82   www.tear.org.au/resources/simulation-games

TANIA's Story

Tania is someone who would never step into a church. She has become a good friend, but our relationship started on very rocky ground. The constant swearing and inappropriate statements she would make to me, offended me many times. But I knew God was drawing her to our community as she had a heart for the downtrodden, and wanted to help children.

She had grown up in a Mormon family. It wasn't long before she was disowned in many ways by her family. She is loud and loves to party and have fun. She landed in our community because she always had a dream to help children who had been rejected and hurt by their families and so Southern Cross Club interested her. She wasn't happy about me not letting her mentor a child. She still doesn't understand to this day why I won't let her, but she is happy to serve and do whatever needs to be done to make the club happen. She is truly a part of our community in every way possible and is one of our greatest advocates. She brings so many people to all our events, gatherings and celebrations. If you said she was going to church she would say, "#$%^ off! Are you kidding? This isn't church, but I wouldn't miss it for the world". She has been embraced and accepted as a part of our community along with her children, who have a growing faith that challenges her every day.

We have been able to create an environment where she is always welcome and yet she knows that everything we do is because of Christ and what He has done for us. We honour and worship Him. When we say we are "praying", she says she is "wishing". At the end of one celebration she was crying. I asked her if she was all right. She simply said, "I know Jesus loves me. I just don't love Him yet". We hugged and I said that was okay.

Since she first came, she has softened. She has gone from someone who would not talk about anything deeper than the weather to now being able to talk about small issues in her life. She doesn't swear on the front steps of the building anymore. Even if she did we would love her anyway. She continues to bring new people and children to all we do together as a community, and is coming to our woman's retreat this year, which is a huge step. It has been three years now, and God is letting her know step by step she is loved and acceptable. She shows most of us up when it comes to joy and enthusiasm.

We are grateful for Tania who is in our midst. She keeps us real and open and challenged about living a godly life in such a way that she would surrender her life to Him. That is our prayer. In the meantime, we are encouraged that the environment we have created allows anyone to be a part of it and feel loved and accepted. We need to simply trust God for the rest.

Luke's story: A child who needs to belong.

We first met Luke when he was just eight years old. He came to us through the Southern Cross Kids' Camp. He was always unique, with learning difficulties and social issues and had been tossed around from family to foster care for most of his life.

When he came to camp he felt that he did not fit in. As a result he created a fantasy world to which he could escape. It was his own place of safety. He would dress up in some type of crazy costume and stay in that character for as long as he could. Basically he would try to be anything but Luke, himself. The activities at camp were all done as Superman, or some evil looking character, or even a woman, as Luke would dress up as a different character each day.

The final night of camp came; the yearly talent show. This was an opportunity for these children to perform in a safe environment. They knew Grandma, Grandpa, the uncles and aunties and cousins would cheer no matter how lame the act was. He quickly realized this was a place where he could live out his fantasies of directing a major play or movie. As each year went by, his plays grew bigger and bigger with a cast of thousands. Each year at camp he was always the star and was often the only one left alive at the end. He usually left the stage littered with bodies, and yes, there was fake blood involved! For a number of years the buddies felt the only way to connect with this boy was to dress up and play along with his games.

By the time Luke was twelve years old, we had a further opportunity to invite him to the Southern Cross Club. This was a monthly club where mentors made a commitment to mentor a child for one year, once to twice a month. Again the club environment was created in a similar way to camp with all the generations represented and working together to create a positive extended family for children who often do not see this in their own situation.

Luke grew and developed in size and age, but he still stayed inside a fantasy world, no matter how much we tried to encourage him out. Everyone worked hard to make sure that the collisions we had with him were always positive and accepting and loving. Sadly, as he grew, the fantasy world he had created was getting more violent, evil and dark.

When he was in year six, I had the opportunity of teaching scripture in his class. I remember watching him come into the class room with the other children, some of whom were making fun of him. His stature and hunched shoulders showed a beaten boy. When the teacher introduced me to the class as the new scripture teacher, he saw me and I will never forget the smile on his face and his shoulders pulling back. It was as if he instantly grew two centimetres. I felt that in his head he was saying, "Great, finally someone who knows and loves me". He sat at the front and let everyone know that he knew the scripture teacher personally. That year I was able to affirm him in front of the class numerous times and make him feel special.

The next year we ran a two-day Arts camp and he came along. I knew it was going to be a challenge when he joined my drama workshop. I wanted to put on a performance that had a positive message rather than a massacre of bodies (which was the only drama he knew). I decided to take a chance and ask him to MC the whole concert night, which meant I could work with him alone and help him script the whole thing. He jumped at the chance.

He spent the whole time reading his lines, walking around with his clipboard and working on how he would say each introduction. As the concert came closer he said, "I am just going to the dress up room to see what I will wear tonight to MC." In fear and trepidation I agreed, but asked him to remember to consider what might be the best thing for an MC to wear. On the night of the concert as parents, families and children rolled in and took their seats, I couldn't find Luke anywhere.

Eventually I found him out the back, pacing with his clipboard. "Okay, Luke," I said. "It's time to get ready. The concert is about to start. Where is your costume?" I will never forget his response. He looked at me and said, "I have decided that tonight I will do it as Luke." With tears in my eyes I watched Luke MC the whole night, with confidence, taking every moment seriously and simply having the time of his life.

I believe that over those six years through creating a safe, loving, family environment we were able to help Luke feel that it was okay to be himself. He is still a part of our community, still involved with drama and our youth events, and he has found a place he can call home. Each year he is becoming more social, more comfortable with himself and more open to God's love. He now spends his time videoing Sunday services and events in a number of churches throughout the area each weekend. I always believed he would become a filmmaker.

One event with 6 Godly Men over 18 months.

My husband and I have always been very passionate about playing a key role in deeply rooting our children in their faith. As Sam turned thirteen and entered his high school years we wanted to help him place important people in his life, as mentors at this time of entering into manhood. We wanted him to find his own faith and choose for himself the voices he would listen to as he becomes the man we believe God created him to be. We asked him to choose five men whom he wanted to speak into his life; men he felt he could learn something from. He chose six and of these, five had been our secret choice, and this excited us. The extra person was a young eighteen year old guy who had been like a big brother to him. We hadn't considered someone so young, but we were open to this. The eighteen year old was very honoured and took it very seriously.

We asked each man to spend a day with Sam, sharing a part of themselves and their faith with him. Each man over a period of eighteen months worked it into their life and made a very special effort to make their day special. Sam loved each experience and they were all very varied. The men ranged from sixty five years old to eighteen years and were men in our faith community and beyond.

At the end of the eighteen months we asked them all to write something to Sam and he would write a response to them. The final event was to invite all the men to the top of our local mountain lookout for a final ceremony. All the families were invited to share a meal with us and were waiting for the boys and men to come back from the private ceremony. No-one else was allowed except the six men and Sam.

I dropped Sam off at a point, and spoke to him as his mother, releasing him and believing in him and who God had called him to be. As he walked along the path he was met by each of the men in turn. They spoke their piece and Sam responded. Then they continued on to the next man. They finished at the edge of the cliff where David, Sam's father, was waiting for them. David spoke into his life the things he saw in him and empowered him with the words that boys need to hear from their fathers: that he had what it takes. David presented him with a symbol of this (which happened to be a Bear Grylls Knife), which we knew would be special for him.

All the men prayed for Sam as the sun was setting and returned home for the celebration. It was videoed and we all got to watch, as a way of sharing with Sam what he had experienced. Being a woman, and not being able to be part of it, was internally frustrating. I had to let my baby go, knowing it was the right thing. I created a scrapbook of the whole eighteen months, with pictures the men had taken of each of the days, and then put all the statements together in one memory book.

I also wrote a poem to Sam entitled, "What's right with you?" and was able to read this to him in front of everyone. It was a great time and a powerful cross-generational experience for my son. Now he knows that in his life he has certain men who will walk with him. Those bonds have formed great connections for Sam in these formative years. He knows he is not alone and that he has what it takes. It was a collision of all the elements in one boy's life, shared with six other families. What a blessing and worthwhile experience.

A car and a Wife: Grandpas Story.

Once a month at Southern Cross Club, for three hours on a Sunday afternoon. During this time we always take some time out to teach them about a life skill, or virtue, that is important for them to consider as they are growing up and hopefully maturing. One particular month was about the "love of learning", a hard one for primary aged children. I asked our Grandpa, who is like Grandpa to all the children who come, if he would share with them about how he has appreciated learning things over the years. He was taken aback at first and said, "It has been a long time since I was at school. Not sure if I have anything to say". We talked about all the possibilities of learning and that we should never stop. I said, "Why don't I give you some time to think about it and when it comes to the time when I would like you to share, I will look at you. If you are up to it, you can nod. If you shake your head I will just move on. I will leave it up to you". I knew that he was the kind of man who needed time to think about things, and he was fine with that and we continued on with the day.

When it came to the time, I looked, he nodded and stood up. I knew it was a risk. You never know what people are going to say when you give them free rein. With a group of twenty five youth and adults and twenty five rowdy children with short attention spans, it could have been a disaster. After all we were talking about the "love of learning" with a group of primary aged children on a Sunday afternoon. Surely this was a recipe for trouble?

Our grandpa, John, has a way about him. It is not fast paced. It might be described as dithery, but something happened when he began to quietly speak. You could hear a pin drop. He started to share that, when he was a teenager, he didn't always like learning, but he did love cars. His dad taught him how to pull apart and put together parts of a car. "In those days," he said, "even having a car was a big deal.". When he had learned so much about a car that he could get an old car and fix it up, he was a bit of a hero with all his mates. Because he had a car, it meant that he was the only one who could drive to Sydney.

He went to Sydney and met a girl, who became his girlfriend, and he ended up marrying her. She was now the grandma sitting beaming right beside him. The room let out an "aughaughaugh" as he continued his story. "So for me, I see there is always value in learning. For me, it got me a car and wife, and you never know what it might help you get".

Everyone laughed and he sat down. Wow! There was nothing more that needed to be said. Our wise, sweet Grandpa had spoken and the children listened intently. There was a collision of ages and words that I believe were burned into many hearts that day. Even if children walked away feeling, "He is so sweet and warm when he tells stories", it is still a valuable collision that teaches the younger generation the older generation have something worth listening to.

My heart is in Cambodia: written by Sam Tolman (13 yrs)

I have been to Cambodia twice now, and I have to say my heart is there. I turn fourteen this year, and I am drawn to do whatever I have to do to get back to Cambodia for the third time, to be with the people in the Village of Trapang Vihear.

While I was in Cambodia I really felt a happy spirit, especially when I was around the kids. Even though they had nothing, they just wanted to run around with no shoes, on bindies, gravel, rocks and glass, and play. They always seemed happy.

The very first time I got off the bus and stepped into the village that we are sponsoring I thought, "WOW", how lucky am I? I am so lucky to even have shoes on my feet, and these guys are lucky to have a bowl of rice every day to eat. I felt so honoured to help this loving Cambodian village. They were all so pleased for us even just to come and share about how God loves them and that He has a plan for them.

After the meeting we gave all the kids a couple of things each and they were so happy. These things included: pencils, combs, rubbers, bouncy balls, etc. They were just small things to us but such a joy to them.

When I played with them, all we had to do was take off our shoes, put them on our hands and hit a ball up in the air. Then for the next couple of hours we were all entertained.

I went to Cambodia to give as much as I could, but I've felt like I have come back with so much more. I went to teach them as much as I could but I feel like they taught me so much more. They have taught me that I don't need the newest and most exciting thing. I don't need as much clothes. I only need one pair of shoes. I don't even need electricity, because they have taught me the simplicity of life and nature. They have taught me that all I need is God!

My heart is in Cambodia. The children are beautiful yet they are suffering. I want to go back and be a part of the solution for them to live a much happier and healthier life.

For more stories see www.collide.net.au

If you have a collision story, why don't you go to www.collide.net.
au **and share it for us all to enjoy?**

Chapter 10

Bringing the Collisions Together

Let's go back to the beginning and bring the collisions all together.

5 elements that are key to a positive Collision.

- We must design environments to re-teach people to play and be together.

- We must breakdown "Silos" and aim for a holistic approach to our walk with Jesus.

- We must empower with language in order to re-think effective ministry.

- We must fight for true community. Where there is acceptance, forgiveness, and unconditional love, which is everyone's responsibility.

- We must create a collaborative spirit, which helps everyone see the value of working together.

Then when we take the four ways in which Jesus grew, we see some vital keys for transformational living, being rooted deeply in faith.

Wisdom: Actively growing in God's wisdom.

Stature: Belonging and living in a community.

Favour with God: Honouring God and recognising the place of awe that He deserves as our Creator.

Favour with Men: Having the opportunity to serve the world around us as we understand our faith and call in this world.

When we fight intentionally to break down the "siloed" mentality

and see the value of creating holistic environments of true community we see that a cross is formed.

Remember that mission must be at the heart of all that we do. It is finding the sweet spot where we can grow in all these areas while fulfilling our missional part in His-story.

When we add the power environment of the generations, we truly start to collide.

I also believe that we have a better chance of transformation when we combine colliding across the generations at the same time as colliding the elements.

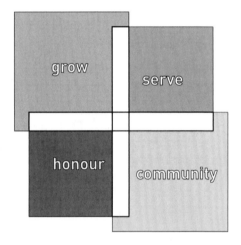

Time to Collide:

Take time with your leadership to ask the following questions.

If we consider the key elements which have been spoken about, what helps to create a positive collision?

What would or could that look like in your home, church and wider community?

Can you, as a group, commit to each other to create/facilitate a collision in the next 6 months?

- Who for?
- Who will be a part of it?
- Who will take leadership to see it happens?
- Who will choose to engage, connect and collaborate to see it happen?

"Though Intergenerational service and mission projects are recommended, there is very little focused literature written regarding why or how to create successful intergenerational service or mission activities"[83]

So…Let's enjoy the journey, and then ***share your stories to help each other along the way*** let's start a "viral" movement that can change the world in which our children live to a place where they can be deeply rooted in Christ. Along the way it just might change us too.

www.collide.net.au

---

83   *Allen, Holly C & Ross, Christine L, 2012 "Intergenerational Christian Formation". Intervarsity Press, USA, pg 230.*